For Colored Girls Who Have Considered Suicide When the Rainbow Is Enuf

For Colored Girls Who Have Considered Suicide When the Rainbow Is Enuf is a 1975 experimental play by Ntozake Shange. Initially staged in California, it has been performed Off-Broadway and on Broadway, and adapted as a book, a television film, and a theatrical film. The 1977 Broadway production was nominated for the Tony Award for Best Play.

Synopsis

Structurally, *For Colored Girls* is a series of 20 poems, collectively called a "choreopoem." Shange's poetry expresses the many struggles and obstacles that African-American women face throughout their lives. It is performed by a cast of seven women characters, each of whom is known only by a color: "Lady in Yellow," "Lady in Purple," etc. The poems deal with love, abandonment, rape, and abortion, embodied by each woman's story, e.g. Lady in Blue's visceral account of a woman who chooses to have an abortion, and Lady in Red's tale of domestic violence. The end of the play brings together all of the women for "a laying on of hands," in which Shange evokes the power of womanhood as the Lady in Red begins the mantra "I found God in myself/and I loved her/I loved her fiercely."

Production history

First performed at the Bacchanal, a woman's bar outside of Berkeley, California,[1] it was first produced in New York City at Studio Riobea in 1975; produced Off-Broadway at the Anspacher Public Theatre in 1976;[2] and produced on Broadway at the Booth Theatre that same year.[3]

According to Hilton Als in *The New Yorker*'s "Critic's Notebook" of March 5, 2007, "...all sorts of people who might never have set foot in a Broadway house — black nationalists, feminist separatists — came to experience Shange's firebomb of a poem. [T]he disenfranchised heard a voice they could recognize, one that combined the trickster spirit of Richard Pryor with a kind of mournful blues."

The play was published as a book in 1977 by Macmillan Publishing, followed by a Literary Guild edition in October 1977 and Bantam Books editions beginning in 1980. Segments from the play were performed in-studio on WGBH-TV's **Say Brother** (now known as **Basic Black**) television series in December 1977, with actresses Paula Larke and Barbara Alston.[4] A heavily edited version of the play was made into an *American Playhouse* TV movie in 1982 featuring Shange, actresses Laurie Carlos and Tony Award winner Trazana Beverley from the stage production, dancer Sarita Allen, and with early performances by Alfre Woodard and Lynn Whitfield.[5]

Awards and nominations

Sources:[2][3]

Off-Broadway

Awards

- 1977 Theatre World Award - Trazana Beverley
- 1977 Obie Award - Distinguished Production, Ntozake Shange, Oz Scott and cast

Broadway

Awards

- 1977 Tony Award Best Featured Actress in a Play - Trazana Beverley
- 1977 Theatre World Award - Trazana Beverley
- 1977 Drama Desk Award Outstanding Lighting Design - Jennifer Tipton

Nominations

- 1977 Tony Award for Best Play
- 1977 Drama Desk Award Outstanding Actress in a Play - Trazana Beverley
- 1977 Drama Desk Award Outstanding Director of a Play - Oz Scott
- 1977 Drama Desk Award Unique Theatrical Experience

In addition to receiving several accolades, the play has been described as a landmark piece in African American literature and black feminism.[6][7]

Film adaptation

On March 25, 2009, the film industry magazine '*Variety*' [8] reported that Nzingha Stewart, a black female director, had acquired the feature film rights to "For Colored Girls Who Have Considered Suicide When the Rainbow is Enuf" from Shange and that Lionsgate had signed Stewart to create a screenplay adaptation and direct the film version of the play.

Stewart, at Lionsgate's direction, approached Tyler Perry about producing the film. However, Perry told Lionsgate that if he produced it, he also wanted to write and direct it. Perry then usurped the project from Stewart [9] and scrapped her script. The shift prompted controversy over whether Perry, panned for formulaic, low-brow productions had the skill and consciousness to properly depict an iconic feminist work. Perry allowed Stewart to remain on in the token position of executive producer of the film.

On September 3, 2009, Lionsgate announced it had acquired the distribution rights to Tyler Perry's 34th Street Films adaptation of the play, with principal photography originally scheduled to take place in Atlanta, Georgia in November and December 2009.[10] The film, which was retitled "For Colored Girls", was released on November 5, 2010 and was written, directed and produced by Perry. The cast includes Thandie Newton, Loretta Devine, Kimberly Elise, Whoopi Goldberg, Janet Jackson, Phylicia Rashad, Anika Noni Rose, Kerry Washington, Tessa Thompson, Michael Ealy, Macy Gray and Omari Hardwick.[11] Mariah Carey had also been cast, but pulled out in May 2010, citing medical reasons.[12]

Perry's decision to make the book into a film was not met without controversy, with some, such as Oprah Winfrey, having expressed doubts over whether the book should be made into a film at all. Others had reservations based on Perry's position at the helm of such an important book in African American literature, particularly considering the controversies raised by *Precious*, a film he lent his name to.[13][14]

When asked if she held reservations about Perry's adaptation of her work, Shange responded: "I had a lot of qualms. I worried about his characterizations of women as plastic."[15] In reference to the film post-production, she stated that "I think he did a very fine job, although I'm not sure I would call it a finished film."[15]

References

[1] Shange, Ntozake. *For Colored Girls Who Have Considered Suicide When the Rainbow is Enuf.* Collier Books, 1989. p. ix.

[2] *For Colored Girls Who Have Considered Suicide When the Rainbow Is Enuf* (http://www.lortel.org/LLA_archive/index.cfm?search_by=show&id=3041) at the Internet off-Broadway Database

[3] *For Colored Girls Who Have Considered Suicide When the Rainbow Is Enuf* (http://www.ibdb.com/production.php?id=3854) at the Internet Broadway Database

[4] "For Colored Girls Who Have Considered Suicide / When the Rainbow Is Not Enuf." (http://openvault.wgbh.org/catalog/org.wgbh.mla:MLA001103) 12/09/1977.WGBH Media Library & Archives. Retrieved 3 November 2010

[5] Tobey, Matthew. "*For Colored Girls Who Have Considered Suicide* (1982)" (http://movies.nytimes.com/movie/260015/For-Colored-Girls-Who-Have-Considered-Suicide/overview), All Movie Guide via *The New York Times*

[6] David Noh (2010-11-04), "Film Review: For Colored Girls" (http://www.filmjournal.com/filmjournal/content_display/reviews/major-releases/e3i57f7ab3b9757aad302472c100f8fda3b), *Film Journal International*, , retrieved 2010-11-08

[7] "Is 'For Colored Girls' a double-edged sword for Tyler Perry?" (http://latimesblogs.latimes.com/culturemonster/2010/11/is-for-colored-girls-a-double-edged-sword-for-tyler-perry.html), *Los Angeles Times*, 2010-11-03, , retrieved 2010-11-08

[8] http://www.variety.com/article/VR1118001644?refCatId=13

[9] http://www.shadowandact.com/?p=9656

[10] "Perry Directing 'For Colored Girls' Film" (http://www.upi.com/Entertainment_News/2009/09/03/Perry-directing-For-Colored-Girls-film/UPI-10721252035492/), UPI, September 3, 2009

[11] . Vena, Jocelyn. "Mariah Carey Drops Out Of Tyler Perry's 'For Colored Girls ...'" (http://www.mtv.com/news/articles/1640173/20100527/carey_mariah.jhtml), MTV News, May 27, 2010

[12] "Mariah Carey Drops Out of Film Due to Medical Reasons" (http://www.usmagazine.com/moviestvmusic/news/mariah-carey-drops-out-of-film-due-to-medical-reasons-2010275), *Us, May 27, 2010*

[13] "Even Oprah Didn't Want Him To Do It! Trailer Unveiled For Tyler Perry's 'Colored Girls'" (http://www.deadline.com/2010/09/even-oprah-didnt-want-him-to-do-it-trailer-unveiled-for-tyler-perrys-colored-girls/), Deadline Hollywood Daily, September 16, 2010

[14] "Lionsgate & Tyler Perry To Make Movie Of 'For Colored Girls Who Have Considered Suicide When The Rainbow Is Enuf'" (http://www.deadline.com/2009/09/lionsgate-tyler-perry-to-make-movie-version-of-for-colored-girls-who-have-considered-suicide-when-the-rainbow-is-enuf/#more-15069/), Deadline Hollywood Daily, September 3, 2009

[15] Brooks Barnes, "Tyler Perry gets serious with new image, new film" (http://seattletimes.nwsource.com/html/movies/2013264517_tylerperry26.html), *The Seattle Times*, , retrieved 2010-11-02

For Colore ... **cide When**

Publisher: LENNEX Corp
Pubmix is a trademark of LENNEX Corp,
Address: Mitchell house, 5 Mitchell Street, EDINBURGH, EH6 7BD, Scotland, United Kingdom
Email: info@pubmix.com
Website: www.pubmix.com

Published in 2012

Printed in: U.S.A., U.K., Germany, Spain, Russia, India, Brazil, China or Australia.

ISBN: 978-5-5107-9178-5

Contents

External links

- Gans, Andrew, and Kenneth Jones. "For Colored Girls Revival, Starring Grammy Winner India.Arie, to Arrive on Broadway This Summer" (http://www.playbill.com/news/article/115756-For-Colored-Girls-Revival-Starring-Grammy-Winner-IndiaArie-to-Arrive-on-Broadway-This-Summer), *Playbill*, 10 March 2008

"McNary, David, VARIETY, "Liongate Acquires 'Suicide," (http:/ / www. variety. com/ article/ VR1118001644?refCatId=13) 25 March 2009. "Sergio, SHADOW & ACT, " How Tyler Perry Got "For Colored Girls...," (http://www.shadowandact.com/?p=9656) September 2010.

For Colored Girls

For Colored Girls	
Theatrical release poster	
Directed by	Tyler Perry
Produced by	Tyler Perry
Screenplay by	Tyler Perry
Based on	*For Colored Girls Who Have Considered Suicide When the Rainbow Is Enuf by Ntozake Shange*
Starring	Janet Jackson Loretta Devine Anika Noni Rose Thandie Newton Whoopi Goldberg Phylicia Rashad Kimberly Elise Tessa Thompson Kerry Washington
Music by	Aaron Zigman
Cinematography	Alexander Gruszynski
Editing by	Maysie Hoy
Studio	34th Street Films
Distributed by	Lionsgate
Release date(s)	• November 5, 2010
Running time	133 minutes
Country	United States
Language	English
Budget	$21 million[1]
Box office	$37,747,016 [2]

For Colored Girls is a 2010 drama film adapted from Ntozake Shange's 1975 stage play *For Colored Girls Who Have Considered Suicide When the Rainbow Is Enuf.* Written, directed and produced by Tyler Perry, the film features an ensemble cast which includes Janet Jackson, Whoopi Goldberg, Phylicia Rashad, Thandie Newton, Loretta Devine, Anika Noni Rose, Kimberly Elise, and Kerry Washington.

Like Shange's play—which is considered to be a landmark piece in African American literature and black feminism—the film depicts the interconnected lives of nine women, exploring their lives and struggles as women of color.[3][4] It is the first film to be produced by 34th Street Films, an imprint of Tyler Perry Studios, and distributed by Lions Gate Entertainment. It is also Perry's first R-rated film. With a budget of $21 million, *For Colored Girls* was released on November 5, 2010, grossing $20.1 million in its opening weekend.

With generally mixed reviews, several critics have asserted that Tyler Perry failed to adequately translate the original stage play to film, while more supportive critics describe the film as his finest work to-date. Shange noted her apprehension in allowing Perry to adapt her work, but was ultimately supportive of the film.

Plot

Retaining the play's poetic style, the film's lead cast consists of nine African-American women, seven of whom are based on the play's seven characters only known by color ("Lady in Red", "Lady in black"Lady in Yellow", etc.). Like its source material, each character deals with a different personal conflict, such as love, abandonment, rape, infidelity, and abortion. The characters are represented by a color: Jo/Red (Janet Jackson), Juanita/Green (Loretta Devine), Yasmine/Yellow (Anika Noni Rose), Tangie/Orange (Thandie Newton), Alice/White (Whoopi Goldberg), Gilda/Gray (Phylicia Rashad), Crystal/Brown (Kimberly Elise), Nyla/Purple (Tessa Thompson), and Kelly/Blue (Kerry Washington). Each of their stories are different, but the characters interact within each other's lives.

The show opens with Tangie throwing her latest lover out of her house. Right after that, as Juanita arrives to piss Frank off with a houseplant, Kelly, who works for child welfare, attempts to visit Crystal on behalf of the children, but she does not get very far. As she flees Beau Willie, she gets some good advice from Gilda. Meanwhile, Alice shows up to beseech Tangie for money, but gets rebuffed instead. Alice goes out to raise money, and encounters Yasmine, who gives her a little money. Yasmine, a dance teacher, is boasting of how dancing gives her underprivileged girls opportunities, a way out of the ghetto, and in to college. Nyla tells her friends in the class about her graduation night with a pack of cousins, then has to throw up. Kelly's husband comes over and arrests two men, one of whom is Jo's husband. Juanita is waiting in Jo's office, with Jo's terrified assistant, Katina, running scared and making tea, and Crystal running late for work. Jo rejects the work of her photographers, demanding work of the highest caliber.

Juanita is let into the office, and attempts to interest Jo in her work at starting a medical center. But Jo refuses, asserting that everyone rises and falls by their own merits. Juanita tries to warn her about the suffering in the community she cannot even see. She asks Jo what the price she has to pay to be so powerful, yet so self-centered, then forcefully storms out. Kelly and her husband visit a physician, who reveals she had an untreated S. T. D. that has stripped her of the ability to have children. So Kelly runs off. Juanita gives condom advice to a group of women, only to be bothered by Frank. She brushes him off and returns to giving the women sensible talk about how to avoid unwanted consequences from sex. Tangie, who works as a bartender, finds a man and decides to show him a night of pleasure. That night, Crystal implores Beau to stop drinking, while he cares only for her accepting his marriage proposal, in the hopes of increasing his welfare benefits. Jo, meanwhile, implores her husband to call her, revealing to us that they'd had a fight that night. At the same restaurant, we also see Yasmine and Bill having a magical night. Alice comes home, grumbling that Nyla moved her box. But Alice shows Nyla the money she has been collecting and asking for, and gives it to her, believing that it is for Nyla's entrance into college. It is not enough, and asking Tangie is discussed, but Alice instead tells Nyla that her god will provide. Yasmine continues her date, explaining that she loved dance more than anything, until she met Bill. Meanwhile, Tangie is having a great time, until she discoveres the man thinks she is a prostitute. She throws him out only to be met by Nyla in the hall. Nyla requests money, which angers Tangie. Tangie correctly diagnoses Nyla as pregnant, which Nyla denies. Tangie relishes her cruelty, enjoying the idea Alice will hate Nyla the way she hates Tangie. So she tells her about an abortionist, and how to find her. Jo is in her house when her husband returns. He claims his battery died, but that does not stop her. We learn that he took money from her bank account for an investment that failed; the source of the fight she mentioned earlier. He feels emasculated, stripped of his automatic right of command of the house, in favor of him submitting to her will.

Kelly's husband comes home and sees Kelly, so Kelly decides to pour her heart out to her husband in a refreshing breath of honesty. Long before she was married, she and a friend were dating the same man, unbeknownst to her. He also gave her a disease which caused her infertility. Despite this, her husband loves her, and stands by her side. Frank attempts to bother Juanita again, seducing her heavily resistant will into taking him back. The next day, Crystal makes an appointment for Jo, then delivers flowers and phone call from Jo's husband. He allows himself to go to the opera, which she loves and he hates, as a means of an apology. However, he is clearly looking at men, desiringly. Yasmine is elated by flowers when Tangie comes to pay Nyla's three-hundred dollar bill. She warns Yasmine about her suitor's intentions, and offers to pay on Nyla's behalf, but Yasmine informs her that there is nothing she has to pay for in any way. Tangie realizes Nyla's gone to see the abortionist, Rose (Macy Gray), which indeed she has. The abortionist is terrifying, and probably drunk. While Jo is at the opera, watching as her husband and another man give each other the eye, Yasmine lets her suitor into her house. He removes his clothes, then hers, and savagely rapes her. The next morning, Jo angrily demands Crystal find a list of advertisers, which Crystal realizes, horrified, that she left in her house. So Jo takes her home. Seeing a male driver in the car, Beau Willie believes Crystal is having an affair. The abuse begins, and can be heard in Gilda's house as she watches the kids. She tries to calm their fears by telling them about her husband. Going to Gilda's house, he captures the children and drops them out the window as Gilda goes to find help.

Jo and an arriving Juanita all serve as witnesses, along with Gilda, to the brutal murder of the children. Kelly's husband interviews Yasmine in the hospital about the rape, to which she gives him a blistering poem as her answer. Alice storms into the hospital to find Nyla with Kelly and some cops. Nyla was found alone and badly wounded. Kelly, walking through the hospital, discovers the grieving Crystal, along with Jo, Gilda, Juanita, and Kelly's husband. Remembering these people and learning of the children's murders, she tells her husband exactly who to go after, and where. Alice storms Tangie's house and confronts her, violently, about Nyla seeing the abortionist. She throws Tangie's newest conquest out of Tangie's house, and they argue about sexuality. They also recite poem and counter-poem against each other. We learn that Tangie's grandfather, Alice's father, had his way with her, too, causing Alice to send her to the abortionist. But Alice was watching her, supervising and protecting her, whereas Nyla was unsupervised. She reveals that her father not only took her virginity, but at fifteen, forced her to make granddaughters with a white man. Finally, Tangie screams that Alice, thinking herself so holy, let their grandfather molest her. She sees Gilda in the hall. Gilda calls her "nothing", then intrudes on her apartment, which Tangie accidentally locked herself out of.

Gilda treats Tangie's shiner with some ice. She tells her that it is not just sex; she needs to find the root if she is ever going to be healed. She knows this because she once was just like Tangie. Juanita comes home to find Frank gone, but he soon comes home. Jo informs her husband, who comes home far too late, about the murder of Crystal's children. Her tears wash away some of her blindess to the suffering of others, (which Juanita had earlier tried to talk with her about) as she realizes how she failed to notice the clear abuse Crystal was going through. Alice and Nyla come home, and Alice forces Nyla to pray for forgiveness while anointing her head with dust and oil. She attempts to exorcise her daughter, to which Nyla slaps her and flees. She tries to seek help from Yasmine, who does not sleep, but sits in bed with a knife, causing Nyla to flee again. Crystal tries to scrub away the blood from her children on the sidewalk, with assistance from Kelly. She weeps for her babies' blood, finding life no longer feels real. It angers her when people walk through it, and Nyla runs through the blood. Kelly recognizes her. Crystal and Kelly get Nyla cleaned up. Tangie shows up with a new man of the night, so Nyla confronts her about the abortionist. The man takes an interest in Nyla as well, so Tangie accuses him of pedophila and turns him away with disgust. Tangie and Nyla argue, again. Tangie admits she has lost touch with reality, and that she is too hurt to love anyone else. Yasmine dances alone, to the poem of Sashita, a powerful goddess of creativity. The dance helps her begin to retain the power taken from her in the rape. Kelly's husband leads her to Bill's body. He was stabbed to death by a woman after he had raped her. Yasmine slaps his face, regaining more of her strength.

Crystal attempts suicide by taking some sleeping pills. While Kelly, Gilda and the sisters wait, Juanita comes in, revealing she had been saved but still needed some rest. Kelly berates herself for not saving Crystal's children because she was wasting her time at a doctor's office. Juanita comes home on Frank's birthday to discover all his things gone, and some of hers, too, in a metaphoric sense which a poem helps her express. As Yasmine continues her classes, and Juanita continues hers, Crystal is fed, then taken home from the hospital, and Jo makes a donation to Juanita. Tangie invites Crystal to a party in Nyla's honor at Juanita's center. Frank tries to come back, but Juanita does not break down this time and sends him away for good. Gilda goes in, forces Crystal to face herself, and accept the fact that she did not protect her kids. She gives her a rebirthing experience. Jo confronts her husband about his infidelity with men, forbids the word 'sorry' from her life, reveals she has HIV, and tells her husband that he is to be gone before she gets back. Jo goes to the party, and everyone is there. Even Crystal. Alice shows up briefly, giving Nyla some books, and telling her how proud of her she is before the music drives her out. Jo and Juanita withdraw to the roof, where Juanita gives Jo some advice about HIV. All of the girls except for Alice join them on the roof, where Juanita says "My love is too beautiful to have thrown back in my face." They begin to share "Sorry" stories, which Crystal wins. Crystal reveals that she is the most healed of them all.

Cast

- Janet Jackson as Joanna Bradmore / Lady in Red
- Loretta Devine as Juanita Sims / Lady in Green
- Anika Noni Rose as Yasmine / Lady in Yellow
- Thandie Newton as Tangie Adrose / Lady in Orange
- Whoopi Goldberg as Alice Adrose / Lady in White
- Phylicia Rashad as Gilda / Lady in Gray
- Kimberly Elise as Crystal Wallace / Lady in Brown
- Tessa Thompson as Nyla Adrose / Lady in Purple
- Kerry Washington as Kelly Watkins / Lady in Blue
- Macy Gray as Rose

Production

On September 3, 2009, Lionsgate announced it had acquired the distribution rights to Tyler Perry's 34th Street Films adaptation of the play, with principal photography originally scheduled to take place in Atlanta, Georgia in November and December 2009, with a planned 2010 release.[5] The film was written, directed, and produced by Perry. The cast includes Loretta Devine, Kimberly Elise, Whoopi Goldberg, Janet Jackson, Phylicia Rashad, Anika Noni Rose, Kerry Washington and Thandie Newton.[6] Mariah Carey had also been cast, but pulled out in May 2010, citing medical reasons (later revealed to be her pregnancy); Thandie Newton was cast to replace her. Macy Gray was also cast.[7]

Originally using the play's full title, the film's title was shortened to *For Colored Girls* in September 2010.[8] In an October 2010 press conference with the cast, Perry credited his full body of work for being able to make the film, stating, "It took everything—*Madea*, *House Of Payne* and all of that—for me to be able to do *For Colored Girls*. Had none of that happened I wouldn't have been able to say, 'Listen, this is what I want to do next,' so I'm very proud of it all."[9]

When asked if she held reservations about Perry's adaptation of her work, Shange responded: "I had a lot of qualms. I worried about his characterizations of women as plastic."[10] In reference to the film post-production, she stated, "I think he did a very fine job, although I'm not sure I would call it a finished film."[10]

Soundtrack

For Colored Girls: Music From and Inspired by the Original Motion Picture Soundtrack was released on November 2, 2010. It features music from the cast, as well as Leona Lewis, and Nina Simone.

Release

The film was originally planned for a 2010 release, but was later delayed until January 14, 2011.[11] However, the studio chose to move the release date forward to November 5, 2010; Tyler Perry commented it was "a serious film that really lends itself to the Fall period."[12] Grossing $20.1 million in its opening weekend, *For Colored Girls* debuted at the box office at #3, behind *Megamind* ($47.7 million) and *Due Date* ($33.5 million).[13]

Critical reception

Upon its release, *For Colored Girls*' received generally mixed reviews from most critics. At Metacritic the film received an average score of 50, based on 33 reviews, which indicates "mixed or average reviews".[14] Review aggregator Rotten Tomatoes reports that 34% of 86 professional critics have given the film a positive review, with a rating average of 5.3 out of 10.[15] The site's consensus is that "Tyler Perry has assembled a fine cast for this adaptation of the 1975 play, and his heart is obviously in the right place, but his fondness for melodrama cheapens a meaningful story".[15]

Early reviews from a private screening by *Variety* and *The Hollywood Reporter* were negative. Peter DeBruge of *Variety* stated that "[i]n adapting Ntozake Shange's Tony-nominated play—a cycle of poetic monologues about abuse, abortion and other issues facing modern black women, rather than a traditional narrative—the do-it-all auteur demonstrates an ambition beyond any of his previous work. And yet the result falls squarely in familiar territory, better acted and better lit, perhaps, but more inauthentically melodramatic than ever."[16] Despite an overall negative view of the film's plot and direction, DeBruge gives praise to the acting of its principal cast.[16] Kirk Honeycutt of *The Hollywood Reporter* also highlighted the difficulty in translating Shange's poetic play to film. He commented: "No, it never was going to be easy, but someone needed to put creative sweat into this one, to reach for cinematic solutions to the theatrical challenge. All Perry does is force conventional plots and characters—utter cliches without lives or souls—into the fabric of Shange's literary work. The hackneyed melodramas get him from one poem to the next but run roughshod over the collective sense of who these women are."[17] Honeycutt acknowledged the talents of the film's actresses, highlighting performances by Phylicia Rashad, Anika Noni Rose, and Kimberly Elise.[17]

Critic Marshall Fine gave a negative review in *The Huffington Post*. He asserts Perry's screenplay is inadequate for its source material, stating that each character "gets the opportunity to suddenly burst into Shange's poetic arias. But the connective tissue that links the various stories ... amounts to a college course in black social pathology—or perhaps just human pathology."[18] Acknowledging the acting talent of the ensemble cast, he states: "Don't get me wrong. The women of this film all shine, hitting strong emotional notes that ring true even when Perry's adaptation feels false ... So let's just say that For Colored Girls is a barely competent film (which is a big step up for Perry), illuminated by luminous performances."[18] Similarly, Lisa Schwarzbaum of *Entertainment Weekly* comments: "The female cast is great, with especially fierce performances from Loretta Devine, Kimberly Elise, Phylicia Rashad, and Anika Noni Rose. But stuck in a flailing production that might just as well invite Perry's signature drag creation Madea to the block party, the actors' earnest work isn't enuf."[19] Claudia Puig of *USA Today* called the film a "strained soap opera" which "has wrung the beauty and truth out of the original in almost every way possible."[20] Mary Pols of *TIME* magazine states that despite the caliber of the cast, "Elise's performance is the only restrained one in the film and her Crystal is For Colored Girls' most compelling character."[21] She concludes that "For Colored Girls feels like the cinematic equivalent to putting a garish reproduction of the Sistine Chapel on the ceiling of your McMansion and calling it art. "[21]

In contrast, a review by *Shadow and Act* was favorable, calling *For Colored Girls* "the best thing Perry has done to date."[22] Perry is complimented on his cinematography, and use of "subtlety and nuance", although his screenwriting is still considered to be the weakest aspect of the film. Like previous reviews, praise is given to the acting quality of the cast, especially regarding performances given by Thandie Newton, Janet Jackson, and Kimberly Elise.[22] *The Huffington Post* journalist Jenee Darden gave a mixed review. She comments that Perry's modern plot conflicts with the narrative of Shange's poetry which was written during the 1970s, explaining: "The film is set in the present and black people don't use the word 'colored' anymore. Watching a character type on a laptop then hearing someone describe themselves as 'colored' a few scenes later doesn't feel realistic."[23] She commends the acting of the cast, stating "Kimberly Elise stirs you as always. Loretta Devine is funny and vivid. Thandie Newton delivers as a troubled, selfish sex addict. She and Whoopi were matched perfectly as a mother and daughter with serious tensions. Singer Macy Gray's eerie portrayal of a back-alley abortionist will make you rethink ever having unsafe sex."[23] Roger Ebert comments that "Shange's award-winning play is justly respected, but I'm not sure it's filmmable, and I'm pretty sure it wasn't a wise choice for Perry ... That's not to say 'For Colored Girls' doesn't have its virtues. Seeing these actresses together is a poignant reminder of their gifts, and of the absence of interesting roles for actresses in general and African-American ones in particular."[24]

Betsy Sharkey of the *Los Angeles Times* gave a positive review, stating that "[w]ith a surgical precision, the writer-director cut [Shange's poetry] apart and reassembled it, using various pieces to create characters and storylines, keeping much of the poetry, writing the connective tissue himself so that it finds a new life, a somewhat different life on screen," and said it is his most "mature" film to-date.[25] Commenting on the acting of the ensemble cast, she states: "Newton's Tangie swings too wildly; Goldberg's Alice, clad in white and rage, never finds traction; and Rashad, as the apartment manager Gilda, the central link between many of the characters, never quite connects, so it often feels as if she's walked onto the wrong stage" but adds that "[w]hatever stumbles there may be, they are offset by moments when 'For Colored Girls' soars," ultimately describing the film as "unforgettable."[25] Mick LaSalle of the *San Francisco Chronicle* called *For Colored Girls* "a serious achievement."[26] He compliments Perry's work, stating "this new film shows a mastery of tone, a capacity to elicit strong performances and also to bring out different colors within those performances so that, when it all comes together, it's not the same note sounding over and over. This is smart, lovely work."[26] Manohla Dargis of *The New York Times* called the film "a thunderous storm of a movie."[27] Dargis states that "working with fine performers like Ms. Elise, Anika Noni Rose, Phylicia Rashad and Kerry Washington, he sings the song the way he likes it—with force, feeling and tremendous sincerity."[27] Matt Zoller Seitz of Salon.com calls *For Colored Girls* Perry's "most problematic work. It's also his most ambitious."[28] He adds that "Perry never solves the stage-to-screen translation problem. But the path he has chosen is as intriguing as it is irksome, and it works better than you might expect."[28] In terms of acting, he praises Jackson's performance, stating: "[s]he outdoes herself here ... It's not just Jackson's short haircut and traumatized eyes that might remind viewers of Jane Wyman or Joan Crawford; Perry gets at the mix of masculine hyper-competitiveness and feminine vulnerability that has always defined Jackson, and links it to the wily, lonely coldness often captured in Wyman and Crawford performances, a directorial gambit of tremendous perceptiveness."[28] In addition, he says Perry "is just as sharp directing Jackson's costars—especially Elise, Rashad and Devine."[28]

Accolades

Prior to the film's debut, *For Colored Girls* had gained commentary as a probable forerunner in the 83rd Academy Awards.[29][30] Lionsgate's For Your Consideration campaign asked to consider *For Colored Girls* in all categories, including all nine actresses for Best Supporting Actress.[31] However, due to unfavorable reviews, the film was overlooked by a majority of film and critic associations.[29][32] Despite mostly negative views of Tyler Perry's screenplay and direction, the film's actresses were almost universally praised, noting several had given award-winning performances, including "[Kerry] Washington, Janet Jackson and Phylicia Rashad."[33] Guy Lodge wrote that Lionsgate should have pushed harder for an Oscar campaign in the acting category, because "[c]hief among them is the extraordinary Kimberly Elise, an actress who deserved an awards break in 1998 for her best-in-show turn in the similarly uneven but impassioned *Beloved*—and 12 years later, is once more the great lost Best Supporting Actress contender of the 2010 season."[29] Lodge is also complementary towards the rest of Elise's co-stars, stating they "produce enough high-level thesping between them to justify ensemble honors that didn't materialize either. Anika Noni Rose, in particular, merits an individual shout, principally for a seething post-rape monologue that lands just on the right side of the film's stage origins. As a sex-addicted bartender, Thandie Newton turns in some of the most alert, adventurous work of her career, while Janet Jackson's tight range has never been more strikingly deployed. And ... Macy Gray's unnerving cameo as a Harlem backstreet abortionist ... further convinces me she's one brave casting decision away from a Mo'Nique moment."[29] *For Colored Girls* has received accolades primarily from African American film and critic associations, in multiple categories including acting, writing, directing and overall production. Kimberly Elise has received the most acting nomination among the cast, followed by Anika Noni Rose and Phylicia Rashad.

Award	Date of ceremony	Category	Recipient(s)	Result
African-American Film Critics Association[34]	December 13, 2010	Best Picture	*For Colored Girls*	Nominated
		Best Song	Nina Simone	Won
		Best Supporting Actor	Michael Ealy	Won
		Best Supporting Actress	Kimberly Elise	Won

Black Reel Awards[35][36]	February 13, 2011	Outstanding Actress	Kimberly Elise	Nominated
			Thandie Newton	Nominated
			Anika Noni Rose	Nominated
		Outstanding Breakthrough Performance	Omari Hardwick	Nominated
			Tessa Thompson	Won
		Outstanding Director	Tyler Perry	Nominated
		Outstanding Film	*For Colored Girls*	Nominated
		Outstanding Ensemble	*For Colored Girls*	Won
		Outstanding Original Score	Aaron Zigman	Nominated
		Outstanding Original Song	Leona Lewis	Nominated
		Outstanding Screenplay, Original or Adapted	Tyler Perry	Nominated
		Outstanding Supporting Actress	Janet Jackson	Nominated
			Phylicia Rashad	Won
			Kerry Washington	Nominated
Heartland Truly Moving Pictures[37]	2010	Truly Moving Film	*For Colored Girls*	Won
NAACP Image Awards[38]	March 4, 2011	Outstanding Directing for a Motion Picture/Television Movie	Tyler Perry	Won
		Outstanding Motion Picture	*For Colored Girls*	Won
		Outstanding Supporting Actor in a Motion Picture	Michael Ealy	Nominated
		Outstanding Supporting Actress in a Motion Picture	Kimberly Elise	Won
			Whoopi Goldberg	Nominated
			Phylicia Rashad	Nominated
			Anika Noni Rose	Nominated

References

[1] Fritz, Ben (November 4, 2010). "Movie projector: Hollywood looking for huge weekend as 'Megamind,' 'Due Date' and 'Colored Girls' open [updated (http://latimesblogs.latimes.com/entertainmentnewsbuzz/2010/11/movie-projector-hollywood-looking-for-huge-weekend-as-megamind-due-date-and-colored-girls-open.html)"]. *Los Angeles Times* (Tribune Company). . Retrieved November 5, 2010. "That should make it another successful Perry film for independent studio Lionsgate, which spent $21 million on production."

[2] *For Colored Girls (2010) - Box Office Mojo* (http://www.boxofficemojo.com/movies/?id=forcoloredgirls.htm), Box Office Mojo, , retrieved 2011-01-23

[3] David Noh (2010-11-04), "Film Review: For Colored Girls" (http://www.filmjournal.com/filmjournal/content_display/reviews/major-releases/e3i57f7ab3b9757aad302472c100f8fda3b), *Film Journal International*, , retrieved 2010-11-08

[4] "Is 'For Colored Girls' a double-edged sword for Tyler Perry?" (http://latimesblogs.latimes.com/culturemonster/2010/11/is-for-colored-girls-a-double-edged-sword-for-tyler-perry.html), *Los Angeles Times*, 2010-11-03, , retrieved 2010-11-08

[5] "Perry Directing 'For Colored Girls' Film" (http://www.upi.com/Entertainment_News/2009/09/03/Perry-directing-For-Colored-Girls-film/UPI-10721252035492/), UPI, September 3, 2009

[6] Vena, Jocelyn. "Mariah Carey Drops Out Of Tyler Perry's 'For Colored Girls ...'" (http://www.mtv.com/news/articles/1640173/20100527/carey_mariah.jhtml), MTV News, May 27, 2010

[7] "Mariah Carey Drops Out of Film Due to Medical Reasons" (http://www.usmagazine.com/moviestvmusic/news/mariah-carey-drops-out-of-film-due-to-medical-reasons-2010275), *Us*, May 27, 2010

[8] *Upcoming Tyler Perry Film Gets New Title* (http://nymag.com/daily/entertainment/2010/09/upcoming_tyler_perry_film_unde.html), *New York Magazine*, 2010-09-10, , retrieved 2010-09-10

[9] "For Colored Girls Full Cast Interview! Janet Jackson, Tyler Perry, Anika Noni Rose & More!" (http://www.urblife.com/the-fame/for-colored-girls-full-cast-interview/). *UrbLife.com*. October 26, 2010. .

[10] Brooks Barnes (2010-10-26), "Tyler Perry gets serious with new image, new film" (http://seattletimes.nwsource.com/html/movies/2013264517_tylerperry26.html), *The Seattle Times*, , retrieved 2010-11-02

[11] For Colored Girls - Trailers, Videos, and Reviews (http://www.comingsoon.net/films.php?id=58777)

[12] Tyler Perry's 'For Colored Girls' to open Nov. 5 (http://amazon.imdb.com/news/ni4108683/) IMDb

[13] John Young (2010-11-07), *Box Office: "Megamind" dominates weekend with $47.7 million* (http://www.cnn.com/2010/SHOWBIZ/Movies/11/07/box.office.megamind.ew/), CNN,

[14] *For Colored Girls Reviews, Ratings, Credits, and More at Metacritic* (http://www.metacritic.com/movie/for-colored-girls), Metacritic, , retrieved 2010-11-06

[15] "For Colored Girls Movie Reviews, Pictures - Rotten Tomatoes" (http://www.rottentomatoes.com/m/for-colored-girls-who-have-considered-suicide-when-the-rainbow-is-enuf/). *Rotten Tomatoes*. Flixster. . Retrieved 2010-11-06.

[16] Peter DeBruge (2010-10-22), "For Colored Girls Review" (http://www.variety.com/review/VE1117943896.html?categoryid=31&cs=1), *Variety*, , retrieved 2010-10-22

[17] Kirk Honeycutt (2010-10-22), "For Colored Girls - Film Review" (http://www.hollywoodreporter.com/review/colored-girls-film-review-32056), *The Hollywood Reporter*, , retrieved 2010-10-22

[18] Marshall Fine (2010-11-03), "HuffPost Review: For Colored Girls" (http://www.huffingtonpost.com/marshall-fine/huffpost-review-ifor-colo_b_778209.html), *The Huffington Post*, , retrieved 2010-11-03

[19] Lisa Schwarzbaum (2010-11-03), "For Colored Girls" (http://www.ew.com/ew/article/0,,20438884,00.html), *Entertainment Weekly*, , retrieved 2010-11-03

[20] Claudia Puig (2010-11-04), "Tyler Perry turns poetic 'For Colored Girls' into a soap opera" (http://www.usatoday.com/life/movies/reviews/2010-11-05-Forcoloredgirls05_ST_N.htm), *USA Today*, , retrieved 2010-11-04

[21] Mary Pols (2010-11-05), "Tyler Perry's For Colored Girls Falls Short" (http://www.time.com/time/arts/article/0,8599,2029254,00.html?xid=rss-arts), *TIME*,

[22] Sergio (2010-10-23), *A few words about For Colored Girls (UH OH! Get ready.....)* (http://www.shadowandact.com/?p=33117), Shadow And Act, , retrieved 2010-10-23

[23] Jenee Darden (2010-10-26), "HuffPost Review: Tyler Perry's For Colored Girls" (http://www.huffingtonpost.com/jenee-darden/film-review-tyler-perrys-_b_774437.html), *Huffington Post*, , retrieved 2010-10-26

[24] "For Colored Girls" (http://rogerebert.suntimes.com/apps/pbcs.dll/article?AID=/20101103/REVIEWS/101109992), *Chicago Sun-Times*, 2010-11-03, , retrieved 2010-11-09

[25] Betsy Sharkey (2010-11-05), "Movie Review 'For Colored Girls'" (http://www.latimes.com/entertainment/news/la-et-for-colored-girls-20101105,0,258800.story), *Los Angeles Times*, , retrieved 2010-11-04

[26] Mick LaSalle (2010-11-04), "'For Colored Girls' review: Poetry in emotion" (http://www.sfgate.com/cgi-bin/article.cgi?f=/c/a/2010/11/04/MV231G5BMO.DTL), *San Francisco Chronicle*, , retrieved 2010-11-04

[27] Manohla Dargis (2010-11-04), "A Powerful Chorus Harmonizing 'Dark Phrases of Womanhood'" (http://movies.nytimes.com/2010/11/05/movies/05for.html), *The New York Times*, , retrieved 2010-11-04

[28] Matt Zoller Seitz (2010-11-04), *'For Colored Girls': Tyler Perry's Misunderstood Genius* (http://www.salon.com/entertainment/movies/film_salon/2010/11/04/defense_of_tyler_perry/index.html), Salon.com, , retrieved 2010-11-04

[29] Guy Lodge (2011-01-14), *The lost contenders of 'For Colored Girls'* (http://incontention.com/2011/01/14/the-lost-contender-of-for-colored-girls/#more-35590), incontention.com, , retrieved 2011-01-30

[30] Breeanna Hare (2010-11-06), *Tyler Perry's latest: For 'Colored Girls' only?* (http://www.cnn.com/2010/SHOWBIZ/Movies/11/03/for.colored.girls.audience/index.html), CNN, , retrieved 2011-01-31

[31] *Lionsgate Awards - Consider This 2010* (http://lionsgateawards.com), lionsgateawards.com, 2011-01-30, , retrieved 2011-01-30

[32] Lisa Respers France (2011-01-26), *Cover story: Where's the diversity at the Oscars?* (http://edition.cnn.com/2011/SHOWBIZ/Movies/01/26/diversity.academy.awards/?hpt=C2), CNN, , retrieved 2011-01-31

[33] Christopher John Farley (2011-01-25), "Does Race Play a Role at the Oscars?" (http://blogs.wsj.com/speakeasy/2011/01/25/oscar-nominations-2011-where-are-all-the-actors-of-color/), *The Wall Street Journal*, , retrieved 2011-01-31

[34] Film Critics *African-American Film Critic Association Winners* (http://entertainment.latimes.com/awards/2010/12/african-american-film-critics-assn-.html=African-American), 2010, Film Critics, retrieved 2010-12-14

[35] *2011 Black Reel Award Nominees* (http://blackreelawards.wordpress.com/), 2010, , retrieved 2010-12-15

[36] *2011 Black Reel Award Winners* (http://blackreelawards.wordpress.com/2011/02/12/night-catches-us-catches-the-critics-too/), 2011, , retrieved 2011-02-13

[37] *Truly Moving Picture Award Winner* (http://www.trulymovingpictures.org/honors/truly-moving-pictures-awards/movie/for-colored-girls), Heartland Truly Moving Pictures, 2010, , retrieved 2010-11-02

[38] *The 42nd NAACP Image Awards - Motion Picture* (http://www.naacpimageawards.net/42/nominees-and-honorees/motion-picture/), NAACP Image Awards, 2011-01-12, , retrieved 2011-01-12

External links

- Official website (http://www.forcoloredgirlsmovie.com)
- *For Colored Girls* (http://www.allrovi.com/movies/movie/v507924) at AllRovi
- *For Colored Girls* (http://www.imdb.com/title/tt1405500/) at the Internet Movie Database
- *For Colored Girls* (http://www.boxofficemojo.com/movies/?id=forcoloredgirls.htm) at Box Office Mojo
- *For Colored Girls* (http://www.rottentomatoes.com/m/for-colored-girls-who-have-considered-suicide-when-the-rainbow-is-enuf/) at Rotten Tomatoes

Tyler Perry

Tyler Perry

at the 82nd Academy Awards
(March 7, 2010)

Born	Emmitt Perry, Jr. New Orleans, Louisiana, U.S.
Occupation	Actor, author, screenwriter, producer, theater director, television director, playwright, entrepreneur, songwriter
Years active	1992–present
Website	
Official website [1]	

Tyler Perry (born **Emmitt Perry, Jr.**; September 13, 1969) is an American actor, director, playwright, entrepreneur, screenwriter, producer, author,[2] and songwriter. Perry wrote and produced many stage plays during the 1990s and early 2000s. In 2005, he released his first film, *Diary of a Mad Black Woman*.[3] In 2011, *Forbes* named him the highest paid man in entertainment, earning $130 million between May 2010 and 2011.[4]

Early life

Perry was born in New Orleans, Louisiana, as Emmitt Perry, Jr. His family consisted of three siblings, his mother, Willie Maxine Perry (née Campbell), and his father, Emmitt Perry, Sr., a carpenter.[5] Perry once said his father's "only answer to everything was to beat it out of you".[6] As a child, Perry once went so far as to attempt suicide in an effort to escape his father's beatings. In contrast to his father, his mother took him to church each week, where he sensed a certain refuge and contentment.[6] At age 16, he had his first name legally changed from Emmitt to Tyler in an effort to distance himself from his father.[7]

Many years later, after seeing the film *Precious*, he was moved to relate for the first time[8] accounts of being molested by a friend's mother at age 10; he was also molested by three men previous to this, and later found out his own father had molested his friend.[9]

While Perry did not complete high school, he earned a GED.[10] In his early 20s, watching an Oprah Winfrey talk show, he heard someone describe the sometimes therapeutic effect that the act of writing can have, enabling the author to work out his or her own problems. This comment inspired him to apply himself to a career in writing. He soon started writing a series of letters to himself, which became the basis for the musical, *I Know I've Been Changed.*

Stage

Around 1990, he moved to Atlanta, where two years later *I Know I've Been Changed* was first performed at a community theater, financed by the $12,000 life savings of the 22-year-old Perry.[11] It included Christian themes of forgiveness, dignity and self-worth, while addressing issues such as child abuse and dysfunctional families. The musical initially received a "less than stellar" reception and was a financial failure.[12] Perry persisted, and over the next six years he rewrote the musical repeatedly, though lackluster reviews continued. In 1998, at age 28, he succeeded in retooling of the play in Atlanta first at the House of Blues, then at the Fox Theatre. Perry continued to create new stage productions, touring with them on the so-called "chitlin' circuit" (now also known as the "urban theater circuit")[7][13] and developing a large, devoted following among African-American audiences. In 2005, *Forbes* reported that he had sold "more than $100 million in tickets, $30 million in of his shows and an estimated $20 million in merchandise" and that "the 300 live shows he produces each year are attended by an average of

35,000 people a week."[11]

Film

Perry received a $5.5 million budget to fund his first movie, *Diary of a Mad Black Woman*, which went on to gross $50.6 million domestically, while scoring a 16 percent approval rating at the film review web site, *Rotten Tomatoes*.[14] On its opening weekend, February 24–26, 2006, Perry's film version of *Madea's Family Reunion* opened at number one at the box office with $30.3 million. The film eventually grossed $65 million. Perry and his co-stars promoted the film on *The Oprah Winfrey Show*. As with *Diary*, almost all of the *Madeas*' earnings have been generated in the United States.[15]

Perry's next Lionsgate project, *Daddy's Little Girls*, starred Gabrielle Union and Idris Elba and was released in the U.S. on February 14, 2007. It grossed over $31 million.[16] Perry wrote, directed, produced and starred in his next film, *Why Did I Get Married?*, released on October 12, 2007. It opened at number one, grossing $21.4 million that weekend. It is loosely based on his play of the same name. Filming began March 5, 2007, in Whistler, British Columbia, Vancouver, then moved to Atlanta, where Perry had opened his own studio. Janet Jackson, Sharon Leal, Jill Scott and Tasha Smith appeared in the film. Perry's 2008 film, *Meet the Browns*, released on March 21, opened at number two with a $20,082,809 weekend gross.[17] *The Family That Preys* opened on September 12, 2008, and grossed over $37.1 million.

Madea Goes to Jail opened at number one on February 20, 2009, grossing $41 million and becoming his largest opening to date. This was Perry's seventh film with Lionsgate Entertainment. At the request of director J. J. Abrams,[18] Perry had a cameo appearance in *Star Trek* as the Starfleet Academy commandant Admiral Barnett, which opened on May 8, 2009. This was his first film appearance outside of his own projects.

Perry next wrote, directed, and starred in *I Can Do Bad All By Myself*, a film structured around his Madea character. This was Perry's eighth film and also made number one at the box office.[19] In 2009, Perry teamed with Oprah Winfrey to present *Precious*, a film based on the novel *Push* by Sapphire.[20]

Why Did I Get Married Too?, the sequel to *Why Did I Get Married?*, opened in theaters on April 2, 2010. It featured Janet Jackson, Cicely Tyson, Louis Gossett, Jr., Jill Scott and Malik Yoba. As of April 18, the film has grossed over $54 million domestically, with $29 million made the opening weekend.

Perry directed a film adaptation of Ntozake Shange's *For Colored Girls Who Have Considered Suicide When the Rainbow Is Enuf*. It was released November 5, 2010.[21] He appeared in the stage show *Madea's Big Happy Family*, which toured the U.S. and was a movie in 2011, written, directed by, and starring Perry. *Madea's Big Happy Family* raked in 25.8 million dollars at the box office, taking 2nd place.

Perry is also slated to take over the role of James Patterson's Alex Cross from Morgan Freeman in the pending film adaptation of *I, Alex Cross*.

Perry's films are co-produced and distributed by Lionsgate Entertainment; he retains full copyright ownership under the corporate name Very Perry Films, and places his name in front of all titles.[22] Perry's movies have seen very limited release outside North America, but in May 2010 Lionsgate announced plans to begin releasing his films in the United Kingdom.[23]

Perry's next film with Lionsgate is set to be *Good Deeds*, as he again will work behind and in front of the camera. Perry will be playing lead character, Wesley Deeds.[24] The movie is also set to star Thandie Newton, Rebecca Romijn, Gabrielle Union, Eddie Cibrian, Jamie Kennedy, Phylicia Rashad and others.[25]

As of June 2011, Perry's films had grossed over $500 million worldwide.[26]

Television

Perry produces a television show entitled *Tyler Perry's House of Payne*, which follows an African-American household of three generations. The show demonstrates the family members' struggles with faith and love, as well as living with different generations. The show ran in the spring of 2006 as a 10-show pilot. After the successful pilot run, Perry signed a $200 million, 100-episode deal with TBS. On June 6, 2007, the first two episodes of *Tyler Perry's House of Payne* ran on TBS. After receiving high ratings, *House of Payne* entered broadcast syndication. Reruns were played through December 2007 before the second season began. The third season began on March 5, 2008 and the fourth season on June 4, 2008. *House of Payne* airs on TBS.

The Writers Guild of America, West has filed unfair labor practice charges with the National Labor Relations Board (NLRB), alleging that Perry's production company, House of Payne, unlawfully fired four writers in October 2008 in retaliation for their trying to get a union contract.[27] The dispute was settled a month later, when Tyler Perry Studios agreed to be a WGA signatory.[28]

Perry wrote, directed and produced the sitcom *Meet the Browns*, which premiered on TBS on January 7, 2009.

Perry has said he may produce more sitcoms entitled *Floyd's Family*, a spin off of *House of Payne* featuring the character Floyd, and another called *For Better or Worse* based on the play and motion picture, *Why Did I Get Married* and its sequel.

In early 2009, Perry threatened legal action against Mo' Money Taxes, a tax preparation company based in Memphis, for running a TV spot that he felt offensively parodied his work, in particular *Madea Goes to Jail*. The ad features a large Caucasian male (John Cowan) in drag, named "Ma'Madea". The offending ad was dropped from circulation.[29]

Books

Tyler Perry's first novel, *Don't Make a Black Woman Take Off Her Earrings: Madea's Uninhibited Commentaries on Love and Life*, appeared on April 11, 2006. The book sold fewer than 30,000 copies.[30] The hardcover reached number one on the *New York Times Best Seller list* and stayed on the list for 12 weeks. It was voted Book of the Year, Best Humor Book at the 2006 Quill Awards.

Stylistic trademarks

Perry always uses possessory credit in his works' titles (e.g., *Tyler Perry's Why Did I Get Married?*). Several recurring narrative themes surface in Perry's work and his films and plays feature predominantly African-American casts.

Criticism

Criticism of Perry's work focuses mainly on a perception that it perpetuates negative racial stereotypes.

Despite praising Perry in 2006, in 2009 director Spike Lee criticized his work when interviewed by Ed Gordon on *Our World with Black Enterprise*, saying, "Each artist should be allowed to pursue their artistic endeavors but I still think there is a lot of stuff out today that is 'coonery' and buffoonery. I know it's making a lot of money and breaking records, but we can do better ... I see these two ads for these two shows [Tyler Perry's *Meet the Browns* and *House of Payne*] and I am scratching my head ... We got a black president and we going back to Mantan Moreland and Sleep 'n' Eat?"[31] When Gordon cited Perry's success among black audiences and asked Spike if Perry wasn't just giving black America what they wanted, he responded, "We've had this discussion back and forth. When John Singleton [created his films], people came out to see *Boyz n the Hood*, but when he did *Rosewood*, nobody showed up. So a lot of this is on us. You vote with your pocketbook, your wallet. You vote with your time sitting in front of the idiot box, and the man has a huge audience, Tyler's very smart. ...We shouldn't think that Tyler Perry is going to make the same film that I am going to make, or that John Singleton or my cousin Malcolm Lee [would make]. As African Americans, we're not one monolithic group so there is room for all of that, but at the same time, for me, the imaging is troubling and it harkens back to *Amos 'n' Andy*."[31]

In September 2009, Jamilah Lemieux made similar remarks on National Public Radio. While thanking Perry for employing blacks in front of and behind the camera and for making work with humor and "positive messages about self-worth, love and respect", she criticized him for making television shows "marked by old stereotypes of buffoonish, emasculated black men and crass, sassy black women." She took him to task for his Madea character saying that through this, "the country has laughed at one of the most important members of the black community: Mother Dear, the beloved matriarch. [...] Our mothers and grandmothers deserve much more than that." She stated that she appreciated that he was dismissive of critics' comments concerning his work, "but many black folks have expressed some of the very same attitudes about your work that white critics have." She stated that blacks "have been fed the same images of ourselves over and over and over because they sell." She felt that his success had been "mired with the worst black pathologies and stereotypes" and called on him to "stop dismissing the critics as haters and realize that black people need new stories and new storytellers."[32]

Lemieux's criticism of Perry was cited and expanded upon by the author Tom Burrell in his 2010 book *Brainwashed: Challenging the Myth of Black Inferiority*. Burrell cited Perry's 2008 film *Meet the Browns* as an example of when "we black people pull the trigger for our own image assassination."[33] Burrell also stated, "...it's not entirely fair to expect Perry to chart a new course alone. His movies and TV shows would not be so successful if blacks didn't have a raging appetite for messages and images that project us as dysfunctional or incompetent. Nothing that occurred during Amos 'n' Andy's radio and television reign could match the words and actions of black comedies like Madea and The Browns. Our attraction to self-demeaning images came way before, and goes far beyond, Tyler Perry."[33] Burrell called for new images of blacks in entertainment and a new vision of black self-image.

Perry (and Madea) were satirized in a June 2010 episode of the Adult Swim animated series *The Boondocks*; the *Los Angeles Times* called this episode "one of the sharpest public criticisms of Perry".[34]

In February 2011, actor Idris Elba caused controversy when he criticised Perry. Elba, who has previously starred in one of Perry's romantic comedies (*Daddy's Little Girls*), lamented the trend for cross-dressing caricatures of black characters – a phenomenon many would recognise from films such as the *The Klumps* and *Big Momma's House* series – describing it as "buffoonish". Elba maintains the view that change should occur in Hollywood to address the recent under-representation of black actors in Hollywood and the controversy it has caused.[35] Elba said: "Imagine a film such as *Inception* with an entire cast of black people – do you think it would be successful?" Elba asks. "Would people watch it? But no one questions the fact that everyone's white. That's what we have to change."[36]

Cultural critic Touré stated in an April 21, 2011 NPR *All Things Considered* interview that "Tyler Perry is perhaps the worst filmmaker in Hollywood" and was quoted as saying earlier that Perry is the "KFC of black cinema".[37]

On May 4, 2011, Perry was satirized by *South Park* in the episode "Funnybot". At the South Park Elementary Special Education Department Comedy Awards, Perry was presented the Kathy Griffin Award, "given to the celebrity most likely to show up". Following the awards presentation, Perry annoyingly remained in South Park, now dressed as Madea, cracking wise and uttering non sequiturs while constantly being given money by Token, the only black student; Token explains that "I can't help myself". The *South Park* writers further satirized Perry by showing President Obama addressing the nation, stating he was going to watch "a Tyler Perry movie. I know, it's embarrassing. But I simply can't help myself." Finally, in a surprise twist, Perry is forever buried, encased in steel, because, as President Obama puts it, "I am pleased to announce that the greatest threat to mankind has now gone forever. Justice has been done."[38]

Responses

In October 2009, during a *60 minutes* interview, Perry was read a quote of Spike Lee's comments about his work and responded, "I would love to read that [criticism] to my fan base. ...That pisses me off. It is so insulting. It's attitudes like that, that make Hollywood think that these people do not exist, and that is why there is no material speaking to them, speaking to us." Perry also stated that "all these characters are bait – disarming, charming, make-you-laugh bait. I can slap Madea on something and talk about God, love, faith, forgiveness, family, any of those."[39]

Perry's work has also been defended by Oprah Winfrey, who joined Perry in promoting Lee Daniels' film *Precious*. She told an interviewer, "I think [Perry] grew up being raised by strong, black women. And so much of what he does is really in celebration of that. I think that's what Madea really is: a compilation of all those strong black women that I know and maybe you do too? And so the reason it works is because people see themselves."[40]

Goldie Taylor, of *The Grio* and MSNBC, stated in an April 21, 2011 NPR *All Things Considered* interview regarding Perry's target audience: "I don't think Tyler Perry is talking to Touré. I don't think he's talking to me, but I know that he's speaking directly to my mother, my sister, my cousins and meeting them at their point of need, and that's what art and filmmaking is about." In the same interview, NPR's Michele Norris reported Tyler Perry had said a week earlier that "Spike Lee can, quote, 'go straight to hell.'"[37]

Personal life

Perry identifies as a devout Christian.[41] He has become good friends with Oprah Winfrey, Will Smith and Janet Jackson.[42] Many of the themes in Perry's work reflect theology and social behaviour indicative of the predominantly African American church culture. Many scenes in both Perry's stage and screen work include church settings and worship styles commonly found in predominantly African American churches, including showcasing gospel music and artists.

On July 20, 2009, Perry sponsored 65 children from a Philadelphia day camp to go to Walt Disney World, after reading that a suburban swim club (Valley Swim Club, Huntingdon Valley, Pennsylvania) had shunned them.[43] Perry wrote on his website, "I want them to know that for every act of evil that a few people will throw at you, there are millions more who will do something kind for them."[44]

On December 8, 2009, Tyler's mother, Willie Maxine Perry, died at the age of 64, following an illness.[45] As of 2011, Perry remains unmarried.[46] He lives and works in Southwest Atlanta where he operates the Tyler Perry movies and TV studios.[47] In August 2010, it was reported that Perry had purchased Dean Gardens, a 58-acre (**unknown operator: u'strong'** m^2) estate in the Atlanta suburb of Johns Creek. Perry was reportedly planning to tear down the existing 32000-square-foot (**unknown operator: u'strong'** m^2) mansion and build a new, environmentally friendly home on the property.[48][49]

Filmography

Film work

Year	Film	Credited as				
		Director	Writer	Producer	Actor	Role
2005	*Diary of a Mad Black Woman*	No	Yes	Yes	Yes	Madea, Joe, Brian
2006	*Madea's Family Reunion*	Yes	Yes	Yes	Yes	Madea, Joe, Brian
2007	*Daddy's Little Girls*	Yes	Yes	Yes	No	
	Why Did I Get Married?	Yes	Yes	Yes	Yes	Terry Brock
2008	*Meet the Browns*	Yes	Yes	Yes	Yes	Madea, Joe (cameo)
	The Family That Preys	Yes	Yes	Yes	Yes	Ben
2009	*Madea Goes to Jail*	Yes	Yes	Yes	Yes	Madea, Joe, Brian
	Star Trek	No	No	No	Yes	Admiral Barnett
	I Can Do Bad All by Myself	Yes	Yes	Yes	Yes	Madea, Joe
	Precious	No	No	Yes	No	
2010	*Why Did I Get Married Too?*	Yes	Yes	Yes	Yes	Terry Brock
	For Colored Girls	Yes	Yes	Yes	No	
2011	*Madea's Big Happy Family*	Yes	Yes	Yes	Yes	Madea, Joe
2012	*Good Deeds*	Yes	Yes	Yes	Yes	Wesley Deeds
	The Marriage Counselor	Yes	Yes	Yes	No	
	I, Alex Cross	No	No	No	Yes	Alex Cross

Play work

Year	Play	Credited as				
		Director	Writer	Producer	Actor	Role
1999	*I Know I've Been Changed*	Yes	Yes	Yes	Yes	Joe
2000	*I Can Do Bad All By Myself*	Yes	Yes	Yes	Yes	Madea
2001	*Diary of a Mad Black Woman*	Yes	Yes	Yes	Yes	Daddy Charles / Madea
2002	*Madea's Family Reunion*	Yes	Yes	Yes	Yes	Madea
2003	*Madea's Class Reunion*	Yes	Yes	Yes	Yes	Dr. Willie Leroy Jones / Madea
2004	*Why Did I Get Married?*	Yes	Yes	Yes	No	
2005	*Meet the Browns*	Yes	Yes	Yes	Yes	Madea (Voice)
2006	*Madea Goes to Jail*	Yes	Yes	Yes	Yes	Madea
2007	*What's Done in the Dark*	Yes	Yes	Yes	No	
2008	*The Marriage Counselor*	Yes	Yes	Yes	No	
2009	*Laugh to Keep from Crying*	Yes	Yes	Yes	No	
2010	*Madea's Big Happy Family*	Yes	Yes	Yes	Yes	Madea
2011	*A Madea Christmas*	Yes	Yes	Yes	Yes	Madea
	Aunt Bam's Place	Yes	Yes	Yes	No	
	I Don't Want To Do Wrong!	Yes	Yes	Yes	No	
	The Haves And The Have Nots	Yes	Yes	Yes	No	

Television work

Year	Show	Credited as				
		Director	Writer	Producer	Actor	Role
2006-present	*Tyler Perry's House of Payne*	Yes	Yes	Yes	Yes	Madea
2009-2011	*Meet the Browns*	Yes	Yes	Yes	Yes	Madea (mentioned)
2011-present	*Tyler Perry's For Better Or Worse*	Yes	Yes	Yes	Yes	Therapist

Awards and nominations

Awards won are in bold

- BET Comedy Awards
  - **2005, Outstanding Actor in a Theatrical Film *(Diary of a Mad Black Woman)***
  - **2005, Outstanding Writing for Theatrical Film *(Diary of a Mad Black Woman)***
- Black Movie Awards
  - 2006, Outstanding Achievement in Screenwriting *(Madea's Family Reunion)*
  - 2006, Outstanding Motion Picture *(Madea's Family Reunion)*
  - **2005, Outstanding Achievement in Screenwriting *(Diary of a Mad Black Woman)***
  - 2005, Outstanding Motion Picture *(Diary of a Mad Black Woman)*
- Black Reel Awards
  - 2008, Best Screenplay Original or Adapted *(Meet the Browns)*
  - 2008, Best Screenplay Original or Adapted *(The Family That Preys)*
  - 2007, Best Screenplay Original or Adapted *(Madea's Family Reunion)*
  - 2005, Best Breakthrough Performance *(Diary of a Mad Black Woman)*
  - 2005, Best Screenplay Original or Adapted: *(Diary of a Mad Black Woman)*
- Image Awards
  - 2009, Outstanding Directing in a Motion Picture or Television Movie *(The Family That Preys)*
  - 2008, Outstanding Supporting Actor in a Motion Picture *(Why Did I Get Married?)*
  - 2007, Outstanding Directing in a Motion Picture or Television Movie *(Madea's Family Reunion)*
  - 2007, Outstanding Writing in a Motion Picture or Television Movie *(Madea's Family Reunion)*
- Nickelodeon Kid's Choice Awards
  - 2010, Best Actor *(Madea Goes To Jail)*
- MTV Movie Awards
  - 2006, Best Comedic Performance *(Madea's Family Reunion)*
  - 2006, Breakthrough Male Performance *(Diary of a Mad Black Woman)*

References

[1] http://www.tylerperry.com

[2] Christian, Margena A. (October 2008). "Becoming Tyler: bill collector turned billion-dollar media mogul was molded from pain, promise and persistence" (http://findarticles.com/p/articles/mi_m1077/is_12_63/ai_n29470264/?tag=content;col1). *Ebony*: p. 4. .

[3] BV News wire report on Forbes rankings (http://www.forbes.com/sites/dorothypomerantz/2011/09/12/the-highest-paid-men-in-entertainment/). Perry is estimated to have earned around $75 million by 2008. "Tyler Perry, Simon Cowell Share Hollywood, Forbes in Common." (http://www.singersroom.com/news/4143/Tyler-Perry-and-Simon-Cowell-Have-Forbes-In-Common) Singersroom (http://www.singersroom.com/company/about.asp), June 8, 2011.

[4] Aitken, Peter C. (2011-09-13). "Tyler Perry tops Forbes' list of highest-paid men in entertainment with $130 million made in a year" (http://articles.nydailynews.com/2011-09-13/entertainment/30173758_1_forbes-list-browns-and-house-tyler-perry). New York Daily News. . Retrieved 2011-11-13.

[5] "Perry, Willie Maxine Campbell" (http://nl.newsbank.com/nl-search/we/Archives?p_product=AD&p_theme=ad&p_action=search&p_maxdocs=200&p_topdoc=1&p_text_direct-0=12C8B2C28A992A50&p_field_direct-0=document_id&p_perpage=10&p_sort=YMD_date:D&s_trackval=GooglePM). *The Advocate*. December 11, 2009. . Retrieved November 5, 2010.

[6] "Tyler Perry Biography – Inspired by Oprah..." (http://biography.jrank.org/pages/2872/Perry-Tyler.html). 2010. . Retrieved January 16, 2010. J Rank's biography website article

[7] Biography.com listing for Tyler Perry

[8] "Tyler Perry recounts childhood abuse on Web site" (http://www.cnn.com/2009/SHOWBIZ/Movies/10/06/tyler.perry.abuse.precious/). CNN. October 6, 2009.

[9] Park Y, Michael (October 6, 2009). "Tyler Perry Reveals He Was Abused as a Child" (http://www.people.com/people/article/0,,20310438,00.html). *People*. . Retrieved January 20, 2010.

[10] "Oprah Talks to Tyler Perry" (http://www.oprah.com/entertainment/Oprah-Interviews-Tyler-Perry_1/3). .

[11] Pulley, Brett (September 15, 2005). "A Showbiz Whiz" (http://www.forbes.com/forbes/2005/1003/075.html). *Forbes*. . Retrieved March 25, 2010.
[12] Bowles, Scott (September 10, 2008). "Tyler Perry holds on to his past" (http://www.usatoday.com/life/movies/news/2008-09-09-tyler-perry_N.htm). *USA Today*. . Retrieved March 25, 2010.
[13] Hughes, Zondra (January 2004). "How Tyler Perry rose from homelessness to a $5 million mansion" (http://www.findarticles.com/p/articles/mi_m1077/is_3_59/ai_111850312). *Ebony*. .
[14] "Diary of Mad Black Woman" (http://www.rottentomatoes.com/m/diary_of_a_mad_black_woman). *Rotten Tomatoes*. . Retrieved October 29, 2008.
[15] "Tyler Perry's Madea's Family Reunion" (http://www.boxofficemojo.com/movies/?id=madeasfamilyreunion.htm). Boxofficemojo.com. 2006-04-27. . Retrieved 2011-11-13.
[16] ""Tyler Perry's Daddy's Little Girls" (2007)" (http://www.boxofficemojo.com/movies/?id=daddyslittlegirls.htm). Boxofficemojo.com. 2007-03-29. . Retrieved 2011-11-13.
[17] http://www.boxofficemojo.com/movies/?page=weekend&id=meetthebrowns.htm
[18] Christian, Margena A. *Becoming Tyler*. Ebony. October 2008: 83.
[19] "Tyler Perry's I Can Do Bad All By Myself" (http://www.ew.com/ew/article/0,,20299647,00.html). *Entertainment Weekly*. August 21, 2009. . Retrieved September 3, 2009.
[20] "'Precious' trailer: Mo'Nique... potential Oscar nominee?" (http://popwatch.ew.com/2009/05/13/precious-traile/). *Entertainment Weekly*. May 13, 2009. . Retrieved September 3, 2009.
[21] "More Than 'Madea': Tyler Perry Changes Course" (http://www.npr.org/templates/transcript/transcript.php?storyId=124459269), *All Things Considered*, March 8, 2010.
[22] Christian, Margena A. *Becoming Tyler*. Ebony. Oct. 2008: 78.
[23] Diana Lodderhose, "Lionsgate brings Perry to U.K." 'Married Too?' to be released on Sept. 3" (http://www.variety.com/article/VR1118019848.html?categoryid=19&cs=1), *Variety*, May 26, 2010.
[24] Kilday, Gregg. "Tyler Perry to Direct, Star in 'Good Deeds' for Lionsgate" (http://www.hollywoodreporter.com/news/tyler-perry-direct-star-good-174431). The Hollywood Reporter. .
[25] Caverley, Alyssa. "Rebecca Romijin Joins Tyler Perry's Good Deeds" (http://www.moviefanatic.com/2011/04/rebecca-romijin-joins-tyler-perrys-good-deeds/). Movie Fanatic. .
[26] Segal, Andy (July 23, 2009). "Perry's greatest accomplishment has nothing to do with business" (http://www.cnn.com/2009/SHOWBIZ/07/23/bia.tyler.perry/index.html). CNN. . Retrieved September 12, 2009.
[27] Mitchell, Gregg (2008). "Writers at Tyler Perry Studio to Take Strike Action – Will Picket Grand Opening and Ask Invited Guests Not To Attend" (http://www.wga.org/content/default.aspx?id=2970). .
[28] Finke, Nikki (November 26, 2008). "TOLDJA! Tyler Perry Studios And WGA Reach Agreement Mediated By NAACP" (http://www.deadline.com/2008/11/toldja-tyler-perry-studios-and-wga-settle-naacp-mediated/). .
[29] Griffin, Dee. "Meet 'Mo'Money Taxes'." (http://www.myeyewitnessnews.com/news/local/story/Meet-Mo-Money-Taxes/KzOnhbVq30ej-QvAe_JT-g.cspx) ABC24-WPTY (http://www.myeyewitnessnews.com/default.aspx), May 14, 2009.
[30] Exclusive: Tyler Perry's Madea Has Scored Again, This Time in Bookstores (http://www.thebookstandard.com/bookstandard/news/retail/article_display.jsp?vnu_content_id=1002382647)
[31] *Our World with Black Enterprise* (http://www.blackenterprise.com/tv-video/our-world/full-episode-our-world-with-black-enterprise-tv-video/2009/05/30/our-world-episode-73/). May 31, 2009. .
[32] Jamilah Lemieux (September 11, 2009). "An Open Letter To Tyler Perry" (http://www.npr.org/templates/story/story.php?storyId=112760404). .
[33] Tom Burrell (2010). *Brainwashed: Challenging the Myth of Black Inferiority*. New York, NY: Smileybooks.
[34] Braxton, Greg (June 22, 2010). "Aaron McGruder's 'Boondocks' lampoons Tyler Perry" (http://www.latimes.com/entertainment/news/la-et-boondocks-20100622,0,7842614.story). *Los Angeles Times*. . Retrieved June 22, 2010.
[35] "Does Hollywood Discriminate Against Young Black Actors" (http://latimesblogs.latimes.com/movies/2011/03/will-smith-black-actors-denzel-washington-anthony-mackie-discrimination.html). *Los Angeles Times*. March 4, 2011. . Retrieved 10 May 2011.
[36] Afua Hirsch (3 April 2011). "The god in Idris Elba" (http://www.guardian.co.uk/culture/2011/apr/03/the-god-in-idris-elba). *The Guardian*. . Retrieved 10 May 2011.
[37] ""All Things Considered" "War Of Words: Tyler Perry Vs. Spike Lee"" (http://www.npr.org/2011/04/21/135610190/war-of-words-tyler-perry-vs-spike-lee?ps=rs). Npr.org. 2011-04-21. . Retrieved 2011-11-13.
[38] Ward, Kate (May 4, 2011). "New 'South Park' references death of Osama bin Laden" (http://popwatch.ew.com/2011/05/04/south-park-bin-laden/). *Entertainment Weekly*. . Retrieved May 5, 2011.
[39] "60 Minutes: Tyler Perry's Amazing Journey to the Top" (http://www.cbsnews.com/stories/2009/10/22/60minutes/main5410095.shtml). *CBS News*. October 25, 2009. .
[40] Issie Lapowsky (October 26, 2009). "Tyler Perry responds to Spike Lee's claim that his work is comparable to 'Amos 'n' Andy'" (http://www.nydailynews.com/entertainment/movies/2009/10/26/2009-10-26_tyler_perry_responds_to_spike_lees_claim_that_his_work_is_comparable_to_amos_n_a.html#ixzz0j7BuSSil). New York: Daily News. .
[41] BY: Interview by Michael Kress. "Tyler Perry, Diary of a Mad Black Woman, "Meet the Browns" Madea's Family Reunion, Daddy's Little Girls" (http://www.beliefnet.com/Entertainment/TV/Tyler-Perrys-House-Of-Payne/Diary-Of-A-Faithful-Black-Man.aspx). Beliefnet.com. . Retrieved 2011-11-13.
[42] "Paper: Entertainers named in steroid report" (http://www.cnn.com/2008/SHOWBIZ/01/14/steroid.raid.ap/index.html?eref=rss_showbiz). CNN. .
[43] "Tyler Perry sending day-care children to Disney World" (http://cnnwire.blogs.cnn.com/2009/07/20/tyler-perry-sending-day-care-children-to-disney-world). CNN. .
[44] Tyler Perry website – "I am so mad" – 07/19/09 (http://www.tylerperry.com/_Messages/)
[45] "Tyler Perry's mother dies at 64; Willie Maxine inspired Madea character" (http://latimesblogs.latimes.com/gossip/2009/12/tyler-perrys-mother-dies-at-64-she-inspired-his-madea-character.html). *Los Angeles Times*, December 9, 2009.
[46] "Tyler Perry: A Hollywood Bachelor's Take on Marriage" (http://www.youtube.com/watch?v=PtnsONBP2fs). 2008. . Retrieved January 16, 2010. CBN Lionsgate news interview with Perry re: marriage.
[47] "Tyler Perry Studios Opens in Atlanta" (http://www.bittenandbound.com/2008/10/06/tyler-perry-studios-opens-in-atlanta/). 2008. . Retrieved January 16, 2010. Grand opening announcement for Tyler Perry Studios
[48] Katherine Q. Seelye, "In Georgia, a Megamansion Is Finally Sold" (http://www.nytimes.com/2010/08/22/us/22house.html?hp=&pagewanted=all), *New York Times*, August 22, 2010.

[49] Michelle E. Shaw, "Tyler Perry to build home in Johns Creek" (http://www.ajc.com/business/tyler-perry-to-build-594061.html), *Atlanta Journal Constitution*, August 18, 2010.

External links

- Tyler Perry Official website (http://www.tylerperry.com)
- Tyler Perry's 34th Street Films Official website (http://www.34thstreetfilms.com)
- Tyler Perry (http://www.allrovi.com/name/p403164) at AllRovi
- Tyler Perry (http://en.wikipedia.org/wiki/Memoryalpha:tyler_perry) at Memory Alpha (a Star Trek wiki)
- Interview with Tyler Perry on beliefnet.com (http://www.beliefnet.com/houseofpayne/)

Trazana Beverley

Trazana Beverley is an American stage and film actress.

She won a Tony Award for "Best Featured Actress in a Play" for the 1977 Broadway play *For Colored Girls Who Have Considered Suicide When the Rainbow Is Enuf,*[1] having previously won a Theatre World Award for the Off-Broadway production.[2] Beverley also shared a cast Obie Award for the latter.[2] In addition, Beverley earned 1977 Theatre World and Drama Desk Awards for the Broadway version.[1]

References

[1] Trazana Beverley (http://www.ibdb.com/person.asp?ID=74369) at the Internet Broadway Database
[2] Trazana Beverley (http://www.lortel.org/LLA_archive/index.cfm?search_by=people&first=Trazana&middle=&last=Beverley) at the Internet Off-Broadway Database

External links

- Trazana Beverley (http://www.imdb.com/name/nm79725/) at the Internet Movie Database

Mariah Carey

Mariah Carey

Carey at the 2008 Tribeca Film Festival

Background information	
Born	March 27, 1970 Huntington, New York, United States
Genres	Pop, R&B, hip hop, soul, dance
Occupations	Singer-songwriter, record producer, actress
Years active	1988–present
Labels	Columbia, Virgin, Island
Website	[mariahcarey.com mariahcarey.com]

Mariah Carey (born March 27, 1970) is an American singer-songwriter, record producer, and actress. She made her recording debut with the release of her eponymous studio album in 1990, under the guidance of Columbia Records executive Tommy Mottola, whom she later married in 1993. The album was followed by worldwide commercial success, *Music Box* (1993) and *Merry Christmas* (1994), with the former becoming one of the best-selling albums of all time. Both albums established Carey as Columbia's highest-selling act, and eventually the best-selling artist on the decade. During the recording of her subsequent release, *Daydream* (1996), Carey began to deviate from her pop background, and slowly traversing into R&B and hip-hop. This musical, as well as personal, transformation took full form with *Butterfly*, which she considered her magnum opus, due to the personal themes it touched on.

Carey left Columbia in 2000, and signed a record-breaking $100 million recording contract with Virgin Records. In 2001, Carey ventured into film with *Glitter* (2001). After being hospitalized for severe exhaustion, and the film's poor reception, Carey's contract was bought out for $50 million, and led to a slump in her career. She signed a multi-million dollar contract deal with Island Records in 2002, and after a relatively unsuccessful period, returned to the top of music with *The Emancipation of Mimi* (2005). It became the best-selling album by a solo artist globally of that year, spurred by the succss of "We Belong Together", which became the most successful solo single of her music career, and was named the "Song of the Decade" by *Billboard*. Following Carey's success with *The Emancipation of Mimi*, she once again ventured into film, and starred in *Precious* (2009). Her role in the film was met with critical acclaim; she was awarded the "Breakthrough Performance Award" at the Palm Springs International Film Festival, and a NAACP Image Award nomination.

In a career spanning over two decades, Carey has sold more than 200 million records worldwide, making her one of the best-selling music artists of all time. Carey was cited as the world's best-selling recording artist of the 1990s at the World Music Awards in 1998, and was named the best-selling female artist of the millennium by the same award show in 2000. With the release of "Touch My Body" (2008), Carey gained her eighteenth number one single in the United States, more than any other solo artist. Additionally, she remains the best-selling international artist in Japan, and holds the top four best-selling albums by a non-Asian artist there. Aside from her commercial accomplishments, Carey has won five Grammy Awards, seventeen World Music Awards, eleven American Music

Awards and twenty-eight Billboard Music Awards. As part of her artistry, she is often cited as one of the most influential voices in pop music, and is credited for her five-octave vocal range, power, melismatic style and signature use of the whistle register.

Biography

1970–87: Early life and struggles

Mariah Carey was born in Huntington, Long Island, New York, on March 27, 1970.[1] The singer's father, Alfred Roy, was of African American and Venezuelan descent, while her mother, Patricia (née Hickey), was an Irish American.[2] Patricia's father had died while she was young, however she inherited his passion for music.[2] She developed a career as an occasional opera singer and vocal coach, and met Alfred in 1960.[1] As he began earning a living as an aeronautical engineer, the couple wed later that year, and moved into a small suburb in New York.[2] After the pair's elopement, Patricia's family disowned her, due to marrying a man of color. Carey later explained that growing up, she felt a notion of neglect from her maternal family, a mark that affected her greatly: "So later I was like, 'Well, where does this leave me? Am I a bad person?' You know. Its still not that common to be a multi-racial person, but I'm happy with the combination of things that I am."[2] During the interval of years in between Allison and the singer's birth, the Carey family experienced personal struggles within the community due to their ethnicity.[2] Carey's name was derived from the the song "They Call the Wind Mariah", originally from the 1951 Broadway musical *Paint Your Wagon.*[3][4] When Carey was only three years of age, her parents divorced, due to the increasingly strenuous nature of their marriage.[5]

"It's been difficult for me, moving around so much, having to grow up by myself... my parents divorced. And I always felt kind of different from everybody else in my neighborhoods. I was a different person ethnically. And sometimes, that can be a problem. If you look a certain way, everybody goes 'White girl', and I'd go, 'No, that's not what I am'."

—Carey, on the difficulty of her childhood[6]

After their separation, Carey's older sister, Allison, moved in with her father, while the other two children remained with Patricia.[5] As the years passed, Carey would grow apart from her father, and would later stop seeing him altogether.[5][7] By the age of four, Carey recalled that she had begun to sneak the radio under her covers at night, and just sing from her heart, and try and find peace within the music.[7] During elementary school, she would excel in subjects that she enjoyed, such as literature, art and music, while not finding interest in others.[8] After several years of financial struggling, Patricia earned enough money to move her family into a stable and more affluent sector in New York.[8] Carey had already enrolled in Greenlawn's Harborfields High School.[9] She had begun writing poems, and adding melodies to them, thus starting as a singer-songwriter.[9] Even from a young age, Carey excelled in her music, and demonstrated usage of the whistle register, though only beginning to master and control it through her training with her mother.[9] Though opening her daughter to the world of classical opera, Patricia never pressured Carey to pursue a career in that type of genre, as she never seemed interested in that world of music.[9] Carey recalled that she kept her singer-songwriter works a secret and noted that Patricia had "never been a pushy mom. She never said, 'Give it more of an operatic feel'. I respect opera like crazy, but it didn't influence me."[9][10]

Towards the end of her high school Carey developed a relationship with Gavin Christopher, with whom she shared musical aspirations. The song-writing duo, however, needed an assistant who could play the keyboard; "We called someone and he couldn't come, so by accident we stumbled upon Ben [Margulies]. Ben came to the studio, and he really couldn't play the keyboards very well - her was really more of a drummer - but after that day, we kept in touch, and we sort of clicked as writers."[10] The two began writing and composing songs in his father's store basement, during Carey's senior year. After composing their first song together, "Here We Go Round Again", which Carey described as having a Motown-vibe, they continued writing material for a full length demo.[11] After Carey's graduation her mother wed once more, which ultimately prompted her to move out from Patricia's apartment, and into a one bedroom studio in Manhattan, which she shared with four other female students.[12][13] During this period, Carey worked several jobs as a waitress, usually getting fired after two week intervals.[14] While requiring work to pay for her rent, Carey's mind and effort still remained with her musical ambitions, as she continued working late into the night with Margulies, in hopes of completing a demo take that could be passed on to record executives.[14] After completing her four song demo tape, Carey tried to pass it to music labels, but was met with failure each time.[15] It was then she was introduced to rising pop singer of Puerto Rican descent, Brenda K. Starr.[15][16]

1988–92: Recording debut and career beginnings

Carey exiting the Shepherd's Bush Theatre after promoting her single "Vision of Love" on *The Wogan Show*, in 1990.

As Carey's friendship with Starr grew, so did her interest in helping Carey succeed in the industry.[17] On a Friday night in November 1987, Carey accompanied Starr to a record executives gala, where she handed her demo tape to Tommy Mottola, head of Columbia Records, who listened to it on his way back home.[17][18] After the first two songs, he became so enamored at the sound and quality of Carey's voice that he turned around returned to the event, only to find that she had left.[18] In what has been widely described by critics as a modern day Cinderella-like tale,[19][20] after searching Carey for two weeks, and eventually contacting her through Starr's management, he immediately signed her and began mapping out her debut into mainstream music.[21] While she maintained that she wanted to continue working with Margulies, Mottola enlisted top producers of the time, including Ric Wake, Narada Michael Walden and Rhett Lawrence.[21] Mottola and the staff at Columbia had planned to market Carey as the main female pop artist on their roster, competing with the likes of Whitney Houston and Madonna, who were signed to Arista and Sire Records respectively.[22] After the completion of the album, titled *Mariah Carey*, Columbia spent an upward of $1 million to promote it.[23] Though opening with weak sales, the album eventually reached the top of the *Billboard* 200, after Carey's exposure at the 33rd annual Grammy Awards.[24] *Mariah Carey* stayed atop the charts for eleven consecutive weeks,[25] and she won the Best New Artist, and Best Female Pop Vocal Performance trophies for her single "Vision of Love".[26] The album yielded an additional three number one singles on the *Billboard* Hot 100, following the four week number-one run of "Vision of Love". Carey became the first artist since The Jackson 5 to have their first four singles reach number one.[27] *Mariah Carey* finished as the best-selling album in the United States of 1991,[28] while totaling sales of over 15 million copies.[29]

Only months after the *Mariah Carey* began its descent on the charts, Carey already began working on her second studio effort, eventually titled *Emotions* (1991).[30][31] The album, as Carey described it, payed homage to Motown soul music, as she felt the need to pay tribute to the type of music and genre that truly influenced her as a struggling child.[31] For the project, Carey worked with Walter Afanasieff, who only had a small role on her debut, as well as Clivillés and Cole, from the dance group C+C Music Factory.[32] However, Carey's relationship with Margulies deteriorated[31] over a contract Carey had signed prior to her signing with Columbia, agreeing to split not only the songwriting royalties from the songs, but half of her earnings as well.[31] However, when the time came to write music for *Emotions,* Sony officials made it clear he would only be paid the fair amount given to co-writers on an album.[31] Subsequently, Margulies filed a lawsuit against Sony which ultimately led to their parting of ways.[31] On September 17, 1991, *Emotions* was released around the world, and was accepted by critics as a more mature album than its predecessor.[33] While praised for Carey's improved songwriting, production and new sound, the album was criticized for its material, which many felt was noticeably weaker than her debut.[34] Though the album managed sales of over eight million copies globally, *Emotions* failed to reach the commercial and critical heights of its predecessor.[35]

As they had done after the release of her debut, critics once again questioned whether Carey would embark on a world tour, in promotion for her material.[36] Although Carey explained that due to her stage fright, and the general strenuous nature of her songs, a tour sounded very daunting, speculation grew that Carey was a "studio worm", and that she wasn't capable of producing the perfect pitch and 5-octave vocal range for which she was known.[37][19] In hopes of putting any claims of her being a manufactured artist to rest, Carey and Walter Afanasieff decided to book an appearance on MTV Unplugged, a television program aired by MTV.[38] The show's purpose was to present name artists, and feature them "unplugged" or stripped of studio equipment.[38][39] While Carey felt strongly of her more soulful and powerful songs, it was decided that her most popular content to that point would be included.[39] Days prior to the show's taping, Carey and Afanasieff thought of adding a cover version of an older song, in order to provide something different and unexpected.[39] They chose "I'll Be There", a song made popular by The Jackson 5 in 1970, rehearsing it few times before the night of the show. On March 16, 1992, Carey recorded a seven-piece set-list at Kaufman Astoria Studios in Queens, New York.[40] The revue was met with critical acclaim, leading to it being aired over three times as often as an average episode would.[41] The revue's success tempted Sony officials to use it as some form of an album.[42] Sony decided to release it as an EP, selling for a reduced price due to its shorter length.[43] The EP proved to be a success, shunning critics and speculations that Carey was just a studio artist,[43] and was given a triple-Platinum certification by the Recording Industry Association of America (RIAA),[44] and managed Gold and Platinum certfications in several European markets.[42]

1993–96: First marriage, *Music Box* and *Daydream*

"The writing partnership that her and I had and I can't speak for her other songwriting partners, but if you could see us in the room I would hit a chord and play a little melody on the piano and she would say, 'Oh, that's nice,' and she would sing that melody and then she adds a little bit to it. I would then play it back and then she would say, 'Yea, that's good' so it instantly becomes this partnership where eventually she'll have a melody and then the melody would prompt her to start thinking about this feeling she wants to put into words. This would eventually become the theme of the song."

—Afanasieff, on his song-writing partnership with Carey.[45]

During early 1993, Carey began working on her third studio album, *Music Box*.[46] After *Emotions* failed to achieve the commercial heights of her debut album, Carey and Columbia came to the agreement that the next album would contain a more pop influenced sound, in order to appeal to a wider audience.[46] During Carey's writing sessions, she began working mostly with Afanasieff, with whom she co-wrote and produced most of *Music Box*.[45] During the album's recording, Carey and Mottola became romantically involved.[47] They wed in a lavish ceremony on June 5, 1993, with several high profile guests including Barbra Streisand, Billy Joel, Gloria Estefan and Ozzy Osbourne.[48] One month later, on August 31, *Music Box* was released around the world, debuting at number-one on the *Billboard* 200.[49] The album was met with mixed reception from music critics; while many praised the album's pop influence and strong content, others felt that Carey made less usage of her acclaimed vocal range.[50] Ron Wynn from Allmusic described Carey's different form of singing on the album: "It was wise for Carey to display other elements of her approach, but sometimes excessive spirit is preferable to an absence of passion."[51] The album's second single, "Hero", would eventually come to be one of Carey's most popular and inspirational songs of her career.[52] The song became Carey's eighth chart topper in the United States,[52] and began expanding Carey's popularity throughout Europe. With the release of the album's third single, Carey achieved several career milestones. Her cover of Badfinger's "Without You" became her first number one single in several European countries, including Austria, Germany,[53] the Netherlands, Ireland,[54] Sweden, Switzerland and the United Kingdom.[55] Due to the song's success, *Music Box* spent prolonged periods at number one on the album charts of several countries,[56] and eventually became one of the best-selling albums of all time, with worldwide sales of over 32 million copies.[45] After declining to tour for her past two albums, Carey agreed to embark on a short stateside string of concerts, titled the Music Box Tour.[57] Spanning only six dates across North America,[57] the short but successful tour was a large step for Carey, who dreaded the hassle of touring.[58]

Following *Music Box*, Carey took a relatively large period of time away from the public eye, and began working on an unknown project throughout 1994.[59] The project was kept very secretive until *Billboard* announced on their October issue, that Carey would release a holiday album later that year.[59] In late 1994, Carey recorded a duet with Luther Vandross; a cover of Lionel Richie and Diana Ross's "Endless Love".[60] By that point, Columbia felt Carey had already established herself as a pop singer, and vocalist, but wanted to to try and feature her as more of an entertainer.[61] Through the release of *Merry Christmas*, Columbia hoped that audiences would buy Carey's material solely for her name and reputation, and squash fears of her being a typical pop singer.[61] The album was released on November 1, 1994, on the same day that the album's first single, "All I Want for Christmas Is You", was released.[61] The album eventually became the best-selling Christmas album of all time, with global sales reaching over 15 million copies.[62][63][64] Additionally, "All I Want for Christmas Is You" was critically lauded, and is considered "one of the few worthy modern additions to the holiday canon."[62] *Rolling Stone* described it as a "holiday standard", and ranked it fourth on its Greatest Rock and Roll Christmas Songs list.[65] Commercially, it became the best-selling holiday ringtone of all time,[66] and the best-selling single by a non-Asian artist in Japan,[67] selling over 2.1 million units (both ringtone and digital download).[68][69] By the end of the holiday season of 1994, Carey and Afanasieff had already begun writing material for her next studio album, which would be released in the fall of of the following year.[70]

Released on October 3, 1995, *Daydream* combined the pop sensibilities of *Music Box* with downbeat R&B and hip hop influences.[71] The album's second single, "One Sweet Day" was inspired by the death of Cole, as well as her sister Allison, who had contracted AIDS.[72] The song remained atop the Hot 100 for a record-breaking sixteen weeks, and became the longest running number one song in history.[73] *Daydream* became her biggest-selling album in the United States,[74] and became her second album to be certified Diamond by the RIAA, following *Music Box*.[44] The album again was the best-seller by an international artist in Japan, shifting over 2.2 million copies,[75] and eventually reaching global sales of over 25 million units.[29] Critically, the album was heralded as Carey's best to date; *The New York Times* named it as one of 1995's best albums, and wrote, "best cuts bring R&B candy-making to a new peak of textural refinement [...] Carey's songwriting has taken a leap forward and become more relaxed, sexier and less reliant on thudding clichés."[76] Carey once again opted to embark on a short world tour titled Daydream World Tour. It had seven dates, three in Japan and four throughout Europe.[77] When tickets went on sale, Carey set records when all 150,000 tickets for her three shows at Japan's largest stadium, Tokyo Dome sold out in under three hours, breaking the previous record help by The Rolling Stones.[77] Due to the album's success, Carey won two awards at the American Music Awards for her solo efforts: Favorite Pop/Rock Female Artist and Favorite Soul/R&B Female Artist.[78] *Daydream* and its singles were respectively nominated in six categories at the 38th Grammy Awards.[79] Carey, along with Boyz II Men, opened the event with a performance of "One Sweet Day".[80] However, Carey did not receive any award, prompting her to comment "What can you do? I will never be disappointed again. After I sat through the whole show and didn't win once, I can handle anything."[80] In 1995, due to *Daydream*'s enormous Japanese sales, *Billboard* declared Carey the "Artist of the Year" in Japan.[81]

Carey performing "One Sweet Day" live alongside Boz II Men, during a special taping at Madison Square Garden.

1997–2000: New image and independence, *Butterfly* and *Rainbow*

"It was '97 and I was leaving my marriage [to Tommy Mottola], which encompassed my life. I was writing the song 'Butterfly' wishing that that's what he would say to me. There's a part that goes, 'I have learned that beauty/has to flourish in the light/wild horses run unbridled/or their spirit dies/you have given me the courage/to be all that I can/and I truly feel ...[sings] and I truly feel your heart will lead you back to me when you're ready to land.' At that point I really believed that I was going to go back to the marriage – I didn't think I was going to leave forever. But then the things that happened to me during that time caused me to not go back. Had it been, 'Go be yourself, you've been with me since you were a kid, let's separate for a while,' I probably would've."

—Carey, on her separation with Mottola which she went into detail on "Butterfly"[82]"

After the release of *Daydream* and the success that followed, Carey began focusing on her personal life, which was a constant struggle at the time.[83] Carey's relationship with Mottola began to deteriorate, due to their growing creative differences in terms of her albums, as well as his controlling nature.[83] With each following album, and her continual established fame and popularity, Carey began to take more initiative and control with her music, and started infusing more genres into her work.[84] During mid-1997, Carey was well underway, writing and recording material for her next album, *Butterfly* (1997).[85] She sought to work with other producers and writers other than Afansieff, such as Sean Combs, Kamaal Fareed, Missy Elliott and Jean Claude Oliver and Samuel Barnes from Trackmasters.[85] During the album's recording, Carey and Mottola separated, with Carey citing is as her way of achieving freedom, and a new lease on life.[86] Aside from the album's different approach, critics took notice of Carey's altered style of signing, which she describe as breathy vocals.[87] Her new-found style of singing was met with mixed reception; some critics felt is was a sign of maturity, that she didn't feel the need to always show off her upper range,[88] while others felt it was a sign of her weakening and waning voice.[89][90] The album's lead single, "Honey", and its accompanying music video, introduced a more overtly sexual image than Carey had ever demonstrated, and furthered reports of her freedom from Mottola.[91] Carey stated that *Butterfly* marked the point when she attained full creative control over her music.[92] However, she added, "I don't think that it's that much of a departure from what I've done in the past [...] It's not like I went psycho and thought I would be a rapper. Personally, this album is about doing whatever the hell I wanted to do."[91] Growing creative differences with producer Afanasieff continued, and eventually ended their working relationship, after collaborating on most of Carey's material.[93] Reviews for *Butterfly* were generally positive: *Rolling Stone* wrote, "It's not as if Carey has totally dispensed with her old saccharine, Houston-style balladry [...] but the predominant mood of 'Butterfly' is one of coolly erotic reverie. [... Except "Outside" the album sounds] very 1997. [...] Carey has spread her wings and she's ready to fly",[94] Allmusic editor, Stephen Thomas Erlewine described Carey's vocals as "sultrier and more controlled than ever", and heralded *Butterfly* as her "best record and illustrates that Carey continues to improve and refine her music, which makes her a rarity among her '90s peers."[95] The album was a commercial success, although not to the degree of her previous three albums.[93]

Carey at Edwards Air Force Base during the making of the "I Still Believe"

Toward the turn of the millennium, Carey began developing other projects, many of which she wasn't able to during her marriage.[96] On April 14, 1998, Carey partook in the VH1 Divas benefit concert, where she sang alongside Aretha Franklin, Celine Dion, Shania Twain, Gloria Estefan and Carole King.[97] Carey had begun developing a film project *All That Glitters*, later re-titled to simply *Glitter*,[98] and intended her songwriting to other projects, such as *Men in Black* (1997) and *How the Grinch Stole Christmas* (2000).[96] After *Glitter* fell into developmental hell, Carey postponed the project, and began writing material for a new album.[96] The executives at Sony Music, the parent company of Carey's label Columbia, wanted her to prepare a greatest hits collection in time for the commercially favorable holiday season.[99] However, they disagreed as to what content and singles should constitute the album.[100] Sony wanted to release an album that featured her number one singles in the United States, and her international chart toppers on the European versions, void of any new material, while Carey felt that a compilation album should reflect on her most personal songs, not just her most commercial.[100] She felt that not including any new material would result in cheating her fans, therefore including four new songs that she had recorded.[100] While compromised, Carey often expressed distaste towards the album's song selection, expressing her disappointment in the omission of her "favorite songs".[101] The album titled, *#1's* (1998), featured a duet with Whitney Houston, "When You Believe", and was included on the soundtrack for *The Prince of Egypt* (1998).[100] During the development of *All That Glitters*, Carey had been introduced to DreamWorks producer Jeffrey Katzenberg, who asked her if she would record the song "When You Believe" for the soundtrack to the animated film *The Prince of Egypt*.[102] In an interview with *Ebony*, Houston described working with Carey, as well as their growing friendship: "Mariah and I got along very great. We had never talked and never sang together before. We just had a chance for camaraderie, singer-to-singer, artist-to-artist, that kind of thing. We just laughed and talked and laughed and talked and sang in between that ... It's good to know that two ladies of soul and music can still be friends."[103] *#1's* became a phenomenon in Japan, selling over one million copies in its opening week, and placing as the only international artist to accomplish this feat.[104] When describing Carey's popularity in Japan throughout the 1990s, author Chris Nickson compared it to Beatlemania in the 1960s.[105] The album sold over 3.25 million copies in Japan after only the first three months, and holds the record as the best-selling album by a non-Asian artist,[104] while amassing global sales of over 17 million copies.[106]

During the spring of 1999, Carey began working on the final album of her record contract with Sony, her ex-husband's label.[107] During this time, Carey's strained relationship with Sony affected her work with writing partner Afanasieff, who had worked extensively with Carey throughout the first half of her career.[107] She felt Mottola was trying to separate her from Afanasieff, in hopes of keeping their relationship permanently strained.[108] Due to the pressure and the awkward relationship Carey had now developed with Sony, she completed the album in a period of three months in the summer of 1999, quicker than any of her other albums.[48] The album, titled *Rainbow* (1999), found Carey once again working with a new array of music producers and songwriters, such as Jay-Z and DJ Clue.[109] Carey also wrote two ballads with David Foster and Diane Warren, whom she seemingly used to replace Afanasieff.[109] *Rainbow* was released on November 2, 1999, to the highest first week sales of her career at the time, however debuting at number two on the *Billboard* 200.[110] Throughout early-2000, Carey's troubled relationship with Columbia grew, as they halted promotion after the album's first two singles.[110] They felt *Rainbow* didn't have any strong single to be released, whereas Carey wanted a ballad regarding personal and inner strength released.[110] The difference in opinion led to a very public feud, as Carey began posting messages on her webpage in early and mid-2000, telling fans inside information on the dispute, as well as instructing them to request "Can't Take That Away (Mariah's Theme)" on radio stations.[111] One of the messages Carey left on her page read: "Basically, a lot of you know the political situation in my professional career is not positive. It's been really, really hard. I don't even know if this message is going to get to you because I don't know if they want you to hear this. I'm getting a lot of negative feedback from certain corporate people. But I am not willing to give up."[112] Fearing to lose their label's highest seller, Sony chose to release the song.[112] Carey, initially content with the agreement, soon found out that the song had only been given a very limited and low-promotion release, which made charting extremely difficult and unlikely.[112] Critical reception of *Rainbow* was generally enthusiastic, with the *Sunday Herald* saying that the album "sees her impressively tottering between soul ballads and collaborations with R&B heavyweights like Snoop Doggy Dogg and Usher [...] It's a polished collection of pop-soul."[113] *Vibe* magazine expressed similar sentiments, writing, "She pulls out all stops [...] *Rainbow* will garner even more adoration".[114] Though a commercial success, *Rainbow* became Carey's lowest selling album to that point in her career.[92]

2001–04: *Glitter*; personal and professional struggles

After she received *Billboard*'s Artist of the Decade Award and the World Music Award for Best-Selling Female Artist of the Millennium,[115] Carey parted from Columbia and signed a record-breaking $100 million five-album recording contract with Virgin Records (EMI Records), Carey was given full conceptual and creative control over the project.[116] She opted to record an album partly mixed with 1980s influenced disco and other similar genres, in order to go hand-in-hand with the film's setting.[117] She often stated that Columbia had regarded her as a commodity, with her separation from Mottola exacerbating her relations with label executives. Just a few months later, in July, 2001, it was widely reported that Carey had suffered a physical and emotional breakdown. She had left messages on her website that complained of being overworked,[118] and her relationship with the Latin icon Luis Miguel ended.[119] In an interview the following year, she said, "I was with people who didn't really know me and I had no personal assistant. I'd do interviews all day long and get two hours of sleep a night, if that."[120] Due to the pressure from the media, her heavy work schedule and the split from Miguel, Carey began posting a series of disturbing messages on her official website, and displayed erratic behavior on several live promotional outings.[121] On July 19, 2001, Carey made a surprise appearance on the MTV program *Total Request Live* (TRL).[122] As the show's host Carson Daly began taping following a commercial break, Carey came out pushing an ice cream cart while wearing a large men's shirt, and began a striptease, in which she shed her shirt to reveal a tight yellow and green ensemble.[122] While she later revealed that Daly was aware of her presence in the building prior to her appearance, Carey's appearance on TRL garnered strong media attention.[121] Only days later, Carey began posting irregular voice notes and messages on her official website: "I'm trying to understand things in life right now and so I really don't feel that I should be doing music right now. What I'd like to do is just a take a little break or at least get one night of sleep without someone popping up about a video. All I really want is [to] just be me and that's what I should have done in the first place ... I don't say this much but guess what, I don't take care of myself."[122] Following the quick removal of the messages, Berger commented that Carey had been "obviously exhausted and not thinking clearly" when she posted the letters.[123]

Carey, pictures with former Island Records head L.A. Reid in 2005, signed a recording contract with Island following her separation with Virgin.

On July 26, she was suddenly hospitalized, citing "extreme exhaustion" and a "physical and emotional breakdown".[124] News websites and programs began reporting how Carey threatened to commit suicide by slitting her wrists the night before, and how Patricia, Carey's mother, hastily called for help.[124] When questioned regarding Carey's suicidal rumor, Berger claimed she had broken dishes out of desperation, and as a result, accidentally cut her hands and feet.[124] Carey was inducted at an un-disclosed hospital in Connecticut, and remained hospitalized and under doctor's care for two weeks, followed by an extended absence from the public.[124] Following the heavy media coverage surrounding Carey's publicized breakdown and hospitalization, Virgin Records and 20th Century Fox delayed the release of both *Glitter*, as well as its soundtrack of the same name.[125] Consequently, critics suggested that in delaying *Glitter*, hype for the project would have largely subsided, and would possibly hurt both ticket and album sales.[126] When discussing the project's weak commercial reaction, Carey blamed both her frame of mind during the time of its release, its postponement, as well as the soundtrack having been released on September 11.[127] Critics panned *Glitter*, as well as its accompanying soundtrack; both were unsuccessful commercially.[128] The accompanying soundtrack album, *Glitter*, became Carey's lowest-selling album to that point. The *St. Louis*

Post-Dispatch dismissed it as "an absolute mess that'll go down as an annoying blemish on a career that, while not always critically heralded, was at least nearly consistently successful."[129] Following the negative cloud that was ensuing Carey's personal life at the time, as well as the project's poor reception, her unprecedented $100 million five-album record deal with Virgin Records (EMI Records) was bought out for $50 million.[116][130] Soon after, Carey flew to Capri, Italy for a period of five months, in which she began writing material for her new album, stemming from all the personal experiences she had endured throughout the past year.[121] Carey later said that her time at Virgin was "a complete and total stress-fest [...] I made a total snap decision which was based on money and I never make decisions based on money. I learned a big lesson from that."[131] Later that year, she signed a contract with Island Records, valued at more than $24 million,[132] and launched the record label MonarC. To add further to Carey's emotional burdens, her father, with whom she had little contact since childhood, died of cancer that year.[133]

Carey performing "Hero" during her Charmbracelet World Tour.

In 2002, Carey was cast in the independent film, *WiseGirls*, alongside Mira Sorvino and Melora Walters, who co-starred as waitresses at a mobster-operated restaurant. It premiered at the Sundance Film Festival, and received generally negative critical response, though Carey's portrayal of the character was praised; Roger Friedman of Fox News referred to her as "a Thelma Ritter for the new millennium", and wrote , "Her line delivery is sharp and she manages to get the right laughs".[134] Later that year, Carey performed the American national anthem to rave reviews at the Super Bowl XXXVI at the Louisiana Superdome in New Orleans, Louisiana.[135] Towards the end of 2002, Carey released her next studio album *Charmbracelet*, which she said marked "a new lease on life" for her.[120] Though released in the wake of *Glitter* and Carey's return to the music scene, sales of *Charmbracelet* were moderate and the quality of Carey's vocals came under criticism. Joan Anderson from *The Boston Globe* declared the album "the worst of her career, and revealed a voice [that is] no longer capable of either gravity-defying gymnastics or soft coos",[136] while Allmusic editor Stephen Thomas Erlewine expressed similar sentiments and wrote, "What is a greater problem is that Mariah's voice is shot, sounding in tatters throughout the record. She can no longer coo or softly croon nor can she perform her trademark gravity-defying vocal runs."[137] In an attempt to "relaunch" her career following the poor reception to *Glitter*, as well as her breakdown, Carey announced a world tour in April 2003.[138] Lasting over eight months, the Charmbracelet World Tour: An Intimate Evening with Mariah Carey, became her most extensive tour to date, spanning sixty-nine shows around the world.[139] Throughout the United States, the shows were done in smaller theaters, and something more Broadway-influenced, "It's much more intimate so you'll feel like you had an experience. You experience a night with me."[138] However, while smaller productions were booked throughout the tour's stateside leg, Carey performed at stadiums in Asia and Europe, performing for a crowd of over 35,000 in Manila, 50,000 in Malaysia, and to over 70,000 people in China.[140] In the United Kingdom, it became Carey's first tour to feature shows outside of London, booking arena stops in Glasgow, Birmingham and Manchester.[141] Charmbracelet World Tour: An Intimate Evening with Mariah Carey garnered generally positive reviews from music critics and concert goers, with many complimenting the quality of Carey's live vocals, as well as the production as a whole.[142]

2005–07: Return to prominence with *The Emancipation of Mimi*

Throughout 2004, Carey focused on composing material for her tenth studio album, *The Emancipation of Mimi* (2005). The album found Carey working predominantly with Jermaine Dupri, as well as Bryan-Michael Cox, Manuel Seal, The Neptunes, Kanye West and Carey's longtime collaborator, Jermaine Dupri.[143] The album debuted atop the charts in several countries, and was warmly accepted by critics. Caroline Sullivan of *The Guardian* defined it as "cool, focused and urban [... some of] the first Mariah Carey tunes in years which I wouldn't have to be paid to listen to again",[144] while *USA Today*'s Elysa Gardner wrote, "The ballads and midtempo numbers that truly reflect the renewed confidence of a songbird who has taken her shots and kept on flying."[145] The album's second single, "We Belong Together", became a "career re-defining"[146] song for Carey, at a point when many critics had considered her career over.[95] music critics heralded the song as her "return to form",[147] as well as the "return of The Voice",[147] while many felt it would revive "faith" in Carey's potential as a balladeer.[143] "We Belong Together" broke several records in the United States and became Carey's sixteenth chart topper on the *Billboard* Hot 100.[148] After staying at number one for fourteen non-consecutive weeks, the song became the second longest running number one song in US chart history, behind Carey's 1996 collaboration with Boyz II Men, "One Sweet Day".[148] *Billboard* listed it as the "song of the decade" and the ninth most popular song of all time.[149] Besides its chart success, the song broke several airplay records, and according to Nielsen BDS, gathered both the largest one-day and one-week audiences in history.[150]

Carey performing "Vision of Love" during The Adventures of Mimi Tour

During the week of September 25, 2005, Carey set another record, becoming the first female to occupy the first two spots atop the Hot 100, as "We Belong Together" remained at number one, and her next single, "Shake It Off" held the number two spot.[148] On the Billboard Hot 100 Year-end Chart of 2005, the song was declared the number one song, a career first for Carey.[151] *Billboard* listed "We Belong Together" ninth on The Billboard Hot 100 All-Time Top Songs and was declared the most popular song of the 2000s decade by *Billboard*.[152] The album earned ten Grammy Award nominations in 2006–07: eight in 2006 for the original release (the most received by Carey in a single year),[153] and two in 2007 for the *Ultra Platinum Edition*. In 2006 Carey won Best Contemporary R&B Album for *The Emancipation of Mimi*, as well as Best Female R&B Vocal Performance and Best R&B Song for "We Belong Together".[153] *The Emancipation of Mimi* was the best-selling album in the United States in 2005, with nearly five million units sold. It was the first album by a solo female artist to become the year's best-selling album since Alanis Morissette's *Jagged Little Pill* in 1996.[154] At the end of 2005, the IFPI reported that *The Emancipation of Mimi* had sold more than 7.7 million copies globally, and was the second best-selling album of the year after Coldplay's *X&Y*. It was the best-selling album worldwide by a solo and female artist.[155][156][157] To date, *The Emancipation of Mimi* has sold over 12 million copies worldwide.[158] At the 48th Grammy Awards, Carey performed a medley of "We Belong Together" and "Fly Like a Bird".[159] The performance earned the night's only standing ovation, prompting Teri Hatcher, who was presenting the next award, to exclaim, "It's like we've all just been saved!"[159]

In support of the album, Carey embarked on her first headlining tour in three years, named The Adventures of Mimi: The Voice, The Hits, The Tour after a "Carey-centric fan's" music diary.[160] The tour spanned forty stops, with thirty-two in the United States and Canada, two in Africa, and six in Japan.[161] Tickets for the tour went on sale on June 2, 2006, with prices ranging from $95 to $150 USD, and featured Carey's long-time friend Randy Jackson as the tour's musical director.[162][163] Carey's performances consisted of old songs from her catalog as well as her newest singles.[164] The tour received warm critical reaction from music critics and concert goers, many of which celebrated the quality of Carey's live vocals, as well as the show as a whole.[165][166] However, critics felt the show's excesses, such as Carey's often costume changes and pre-filmed clips, were unnecessary distractions.[165] The tour proved successful, with Carey playing to over 60,000 fans in the two stop in Tunis alone.[167] Midway through the tour, Carey booked a two-night concert engagement in Hong Kong, which was scheduled to take place following her Japanese shows.[168] The shows were cancelled, however, after tickets went on sale. According to Carey's then-manager Benny Medina, the cancellation was due to the concert promoter's refusal to pay Carey her agreed-upon compensation.[168] The promoter instead blamed poor ticket sales (allegedly, only 4,000 tickets had sold) and "Carey's outrageous demands".[169] Carey ultimately sued the promoter, claiming $1 million in damages due to the concert's abrupt cancellation.[170]

2007–09: *E=MC²*, second marriage, and acting breakthrough

Carey and her dancers performing "Touch My Body" on *Good Morning America* on April 25, 2008

By spring 2007, Carey had begun to work on her eleventh studio album, *E=MC²*, in a private villa in Anguilla.[171] When asked regarding the album title's meaning, Carey said "Einstein's theory? Physics? *Me?* Hello! ...Of course I'm poking fun."[172] She characterized it as "*Emancipation of Mimi* to the second power", and said that she was "freer" on this album than any other.[172] Although *E=MC²* was well received by most critics,[173] some of them criticized it for being very similar to the formula used on *The Emancipation of Mimi*.[174] Two weeks before the album's release, "Touch My Body", the record's lead single reached the top position on the *Billboard* Hot 100, becoming Carey's eighteenth number one and making her the solo artist with the most number one singles in United States history, surpassing the record held by Elvis Presley.[175] Additionally, it gave Carey her 79th week atop the Hot 100, tying her with Presley as the artist with the most weeks at number one in the *Billboard* chart history."[176] *E=MC²* debuted at number one on the *Billboard* 200 with 463,000 copies sold, the biggest opening week sales of her career.[35] With six number one albums, Carey is now tied with Britney Spears and Janet Jackson in the United States for the third most number one albums for a female artist, behind Madonna with seven and Barbra Streisand's nine chart toppers.[35] In 2008, *Billboard* magazine ranked her at number six on the "Billboard Hot 100 All-Time Top Artists", making Carey the second most successful female artist in the history of the *Billboard* Hot 100 chart.[177] Carey and actor/comedian Nick Cannon met while they shot her music video for her second single, "Bye Bye", on an island off the coast of Antigua.[178] On April 30, 2008, Carey married Cannon at her private estate on Windermere Island in The Bahamas.[179][180] Carey had a cameo appearance in Adam Sandler's 2008 film *You Don't Mess with the Zohan*, playing herself.[88] On January 20, 2009, Carey performed "Hero" at the Neighborhood Inaugural Ball after Barack Obama was sworn as America's first African-American president.[181] On July 7, 2009, Carey – alongside Trey Lorenz – performed her version of The Jackson 5 song "I'll Be There" at the memorial service for Michael Jackson.[182] At the sight of Jackson's casket, Carey's voice, overwhelmed with emotion, cracked in the opening line of the song.[183] She later apologized on *The Today Show*, explaining how she did her best effort despite the circumstances.[183]

Carey performing "Hero" live during The Neighborhood Inaugural Ball for President Obama in Washington D.C..

In 2009, she appeared as a social worker in *Precious*, the movie adaptation of the 1996 novel *Push* by Sapphire. The film garnered mostly positive reviews from critics, as has Carey's performance.[184] *Variety* described her acting as "pitch-perfect".[185] *Precious* won awards at both the Sundance Film Festival and the Toronto Film Festival, receiving top honors there.[186][187] In January 2010, Carey won the Breakthrough Actress Performance Award for her role in *Precious* at the Palm Springs International Film Festival.[188] September 25, 2009, Carey's twelfth studio album, *Memoirs of an Imperfect Angel*, was released. Reception for the album was generally positive, but mixed in certain aspects; Stephen Thomas Erlewine of Allmusic called it "her most interesting album in a decade",[189] while Jon Caramanica from

The New York Times criticized Carey's vocal performances, decrying her overuse of her softer vocal registers at the expense of her more powerful lower and upper registers.[190] Commercially, the album debuted at number three on the *Billboard* 200, and became the lowest-selling studio album of her career.[191] The album's lead single, "Obsessed", became her 40th entry on the *Billboard* Hot 100 and her highest debut on the chart since "My All" in 1998.[192] The song debuted at number eleven and peaked at number seven on the chart, and became Carey's 27th US top-ten hit, tying her with Elton John and Janet Jackson as the fifth most top-ten hits.[192] Within hours after the song's release, various outlets speculated that its target was rapper Eminem, in response to his song "Bagpipes from Baghdad", in which he taunted Carey's husband, Nick Cannon.[193] According to MTV, Carey alludes to drug problems in "Obsessed", which Eminem opened up about on his sixth studio album, *Relapse*.[194] The album's follow-up single, a cover of Foreigner's "I Want to Know What Love Is", failed to achieve any significant chart success in the United States, or much throughout Europe, but managed to break airplay records in Brazil. The song spent 27 weeks atop the Brasil Hot 100 Airplay, making it the longest running song in the chart's history.[195] On December 31, 2009, Carey embarked her seventh concert tour, Angels Advocate Tour, which visited the United States and Canada.[196] Though stateside, the tour spanned few international dates, such as in Brazil and Singapore, where Carey played to over 100,000 spectators.[197] On January 30, 2010, it was announced that Carey would release a remix album of *Memoirs of an Imperfect Angel*; titled *Angels Advocate* (an R&B remix album featuring a collection of newly remixed duets with some of Carey's favorite artists).[198] The album was slated for a March 30, 2010 release, but were eventually cancelled.[199]

2010–present: *Merry Christmas II You*, motherhood and new album

Carey performing live in "All I Want for Christmas Is You" live at the Walt Disney World Resort on December 3, 2010

Following the cancellation of the *Angels Advocate*, it was announced that Carey would return to the studio to start work on her thirteenth studio album.[200] It was later revealed that it would be her second Christmas album, the follow-up to *Merry Christmas* (1994), which became the best-selling Holiday album of all time.[63] Long time collaborators for the project include Jermaine Dupri, Johntá Austin, Bryan-Michael Cox and Randy Jackson, as well as new collaborators such as Marc Shaiman.[201] Dupri stated that a single would be released alongside the album before the year's end.[201] During a press conference in Seoul, South Korea, in August 2010, Island Def Jam executive Matt Voss announced that the album would be out on November 2, 2010.[202] and would include six new songs and a remix of her classic hit "All I Want for Christmas Is You".[203] The album, titled *Merry Christmas II You*, was released alongside an accompanying DVD, and was sent to retailers on November 2, 2010.[204] *Merry Christmas II You* debuted at number four on the *Billboard* 200 with sales of 56,000 copies, surpassing the opening week sales of Carey's previous holiday album of 45,000 copies 16 years prior.[205] It also became Carey's 16th top ten album in the United States.[205] The album debuted at number one on the R&B/Hip-Hop Albums chart, making it only the second Christmas album to top this chart.[206]

In May 2010, Carey dropped out of her planned appearance in *For Colored Girls*, the film adaptation of the play *For Colored Girls Who Have Considered Suicide When the Rainbow Is Enuf*, citing medical reasons.[207] After much media speculation, Carey confirmed on October 28, 2010 that she and Cannon were expecting a baby, and that she would be due in the Spring of 2011.[208] Carey also revealed that she had been pregnant shortly after her wedding with Cannon, but she miscarried.[209] On April 30, 2011, the couple's third wedding anniversary, Carey gave birth to fraternal twins via C-section.[210] The twins were named Monroe, after Marilyn Monroe, and Moroccan Scott, after Cannon proposed to Carey in her Moroccan-style room; Scott is Cannon's middle name and his grandmother's maiden name.[211] On February 11, 2011, Carey announced on HSN, that she recorded a duet with Tony Bennett for his upcoming "Duets" album, titled "When Do The Bells Ring For Me".[212] Following the birth of their children, Cannon revealed during an interview with *Billboard* that Carey had already begun working on a new record.[213] Cannon said "She's been working away, and we have a studio in the crib, and [the pregnancy] has totally inspired her on so many different levels. You're definitely gonna see some new phenomenal music from Mariah" and assured

Carey would plan on releasing it by the end of the year.[214] In October 2011, Carey announced that she re-recorded her song "All I Want for Christmas Is You" with Justin Bieber as a duet for his Christmas album, *Under the Mistletoe*.[215][216] On November 5, 2011, Carey and Bieber filmed a music video for the duet at the Macy's in New York City.[217] On October 21, 2011, a pre-taped interview with Barbara Walters aired on ABC's 20/20, during the interview Carey and Cannon allowed the cameras to photograph/film twins Moroccan and Monroe for the first time ever.[218] In November 2011, Carey was included in the remix to the mixtape single "Warning" by Uncle Murda, the remix also features 50 Cent and Young Jeezy.[219] That same month, Carey announced that she and John Legend collaborated on a duet, "When Christmas Comes", which was originally part of Carey's 2010 holiday album "Merry Christmas II You".[220]

Artistry

Musical style

Carey at Edwards Air Force Base during the making of "I Still Believe" video in 1998

Love is the subject of the majority of Carey's lyrics, although she has written about themes such as racism, social alienation, death, world hunger, and spirituality. She has said that much of her work is partly autobiographical, but *Time* magazine wrote: "If only Mariah Carey's music had the drama of her life. Her songs are often sugary and artificial—NutraSweet soul. But her life has passion and conflict," applying it to the first stages of her career. He commented that as her album's progressed, so too her songwriting and music blossomed into more mature and meaningful material.[221] Jim Faber of the *New York Daily News*, made similar comments, "For Carey, vocalizing is all about the performance, not the emotions that inspired it. Singing, to her, represents a physical challenge, not an emotional unburdening."[222] While reviewing *Music Box*, Stephen Holden from *Rolling Stone* commented that Carey sang with "sustained passion", while *Entertainment Weekly*'s Arion Berger wrote that during some vocal moments, Carey becomes "too overwhelmed to put her passion into words."[223] In 2001, *The Village Voice* wrote in regards to what they considered Carey's "centerless ballads", writing, "Carey's Strawberry Shortcake soul still provides the template with which teen-pop cuties draw curlicues around those centerless [Diane] Warren ballads [...] it's largely because of [Blige] that the new R&B demands a greater range of emotional expression, smarter poetry, more from-the-gut testifying, and less unnecessary notes than the squeaky-clean and just plain squeaky Mariah era. Nowadays it's the Christina Aguileras and Jessica Simpsons who awkwardly oversing, while the women with roof-raising lung power keep it in check when tune or lyric demands."[224]

Carey's output makes use of electronic instruments such as drum machines,[143] keyboards and synthesizers.[225] Many of her songs contain piano-driven melodies,[226] as she was given piano lessons when she was six years old..[5] Carey said that she cannot read sheet music and prefers to collaborate with a pianist when composing her material, but feels that it is easier to experiment with faster and less conventional melodies and chord progressions using this technique.[5] While Carey learned to play the piano at a young age, and incorporates several ranges of production and instrumentation into her music, she has maintained that her voice has always been her most important asset: "My voice is my instrument; it always has been."[93] Carey began commissioning remixes of her material early in her career and helped to spearhead the practice of recording entirely new vocals for remixes.[227] Disc jockey David Morales has collaborated with Carey on several occasions, starting with "Dreamlover" (1993), which popularized the tradition of remixing R&B songs into house records, and which *Slant* magazine named one of the greatest dance songs of all time.[228] From "Fantasy" (1995) onward, Carey enlisted both hip-hop and house producers to re-structure her album compositions.[80] *Entertainment Weekly* included two remixes of "Fantasy" on a list of Carey's greatest recordings compiled in 2005: a National Dance Music Award-winning remix produced by Morales, and a Sean Combs production featuring rapper Ol' Dirty Bastard.[229] The latter has been credited with popularizing the R&B/hip-hop collaboration trend that has continued into the 2000s, through artists such as Ashanti and Beyoncé.[227] Combs said that Carey "knows the importance of mixes, so you feel like you're with an artist who appreciates your work—an artist who wants to come up with something with you".[230]

Voice and timbre

"I have nodules on my vocal cords. My mother says I've had them since I was a kid. That's why I have the high register and the belting register and I can still be husky. The only thing that really affects my voice is sleep. Sometimes if I'm exhausted, I can't hit the really high notes. My doctors showed me my vocal cords and why I can hit those high notes. It's a certain part of the cord that not many people use—the very top. My natural voice is low. I have a raspy voice. I'm really more of an alto. But my airy voice can be high if I'm rested. [...] When I was little, I'd talk in this really high whisper, and my mom would be like, 'You're being ridiculous'. I thought if I can talk like that I can sing like that. So I started [she goes higher and higher and higher] just messing around with it. I'd practice and practice, and she'd be like, "You're gonna hurt yourself." I'd tell her, It doesn't hurt. If I were to try and belt two octaves lower than that, that would be a strain."

—Carey, on the background and her usage of the whistle register[101]

Mariah Carey possesses a 5-octave vocal range,[231][232][130] and has the ability to reach notes beyond the 7th octave.[233][234] She was ranked first in a 2003 MTV and *Blender* magazine countdown of the 22 Greatest Voices in Music, as voted by fans and readers in an online poll. Carey said of the poll, "What it really means is voice of the MTV generation. Of course, it's an enormous compliment, but I don't feel that way about myself."[235] She also placed second in *Cove* magazine's list of "The 100 Outstanding Pop Vocalists".[236]

Regarding her voice type, Carey said that she is alto, while French-American baritone and singing teacher in the Conservatoire de Paris Malcolm Walker states that she is light lyric soprano, "because the upper register is much more healthier [*sic*] than the lower register."[237] However, within contemporary forms of music, singers are classified by the style of music they sing. There is currently no authoritative voice classification system within non-classical music.[238] Attempts have been made to adopt classical voice type terms to other forms of singing, but they are controversial,[238] because the development of classic voice categorizations were made with the understanding that the singer would amplify his or her voice with their natural resonators, without a microphone.[239] Author Chris Nickson described Carey's Legato in depth while discussing *Music Box*, describing how Carey is able to "keep the tunes softness and sweetness, without resorting to volume. Carey's vocals are defined as soft and controlled, managing to maintain the delicate balance in a manner that seems effortless."[240]

Baritone Malcolm Walker[237] as well as music critic Stephen Holden of *The New York Times*[241] and vocal pedagogue Jeannette Lo Vetri describes Carey's voice as "pure, full, rounded and warm", adding that belting and head voices has a great brightness.[241][238] Malcolm Walker praise her belting voice, saying it "works very well" and states that Carey "passes easily in head voice. It's her true voice."[237] The middle register is "ample and full"[237][241][238] and the voice resonates with strong vibrato.[241][238] Jon Pareles, of *The New York Times*, describes Carey's lower register as "rich" and "husky",[242] on the other hand, Walker,[237] Holden,[241] and Lo Vetri[238] state it's "tired", "distended" in its lowest parts. Carey also possesses a "whisper register". In an interview with the singer, Ron Givens of *Entertainment Weekly* described it this way, "In one brief swoop, she seems to squeal and roar at the same time: whisper register."[243] Additionally, towards the late 1990s, Carey began incorporating breathy vocals into her material, usually beginning the song and then building up to a "full throated" climax.[244] Tim Levell from the BBC News described her vocals as "sultry close-to-the-mic breathiness"[244], while *USA Today*'s Elysa Gardner wrote "it's impossible to deny the impact her vocal style, a florid blend of breathy riffing and resonant belting, has had on today's young pop and R&B stars."[245]

Voice experts praise Carey's vocal technique, stating that she can deliver very fast and controlled staccatos[241][238] "always keeps a neutral larynx position—except sometimes in her lower register" and "glides effortlessly from bottom to top and vice versa."[238] Her mastery of melismas and legato is also very praised.[241][238][62] Malcolm Walker adds her vocal lines are "very well led, especially in piano register."[237] According to Spanish soprano Montserrat Caballé, "Carey is such a musician. Perfect timing, divine accuracy, subtle and refined phrasing, melismas always connected to the rhythm and structure of song, infaillible ability to etablish and resolving musical ideas and theme and effortless combination of climax and resolve."[246] Jon Pareles also praise her musicianship, writing, "she can linger over sensual turns, ... syncopate like a scat singer [and sing] with startlingly exact pitch."[242]

Influences

Carey has said that from childhood she has been influenced by R&B and soul musicians such as Billie Holiday and Sarah Vaughan.[247] Her music contains strong influences of gospel music, and she credits The Clark Sisters, Shirley Caesar and Edwin Hawkins as the most influential in her early years.[247] When Carey incorporated hip-hop into her sound, speculation arose that she was making an attempt to take advantage of the genre's popularity, but she told *Newsweek*, "People just don't understand. I grew up with this music".[248] She has expressed appreciation for rappers such as The Sugarhill Gang, Eric B. & Rakim, the Wu-Tang Clan, The Notorious B.I.G. and Mobb Deep, with whom she collaborated on the single "The Roof (Back in Time)" (1998).[101] Carey was heavily influenced by Minnie Riperton, and began experimenting with the whistle register due to her original practice of the range.[101]

During Carey's career, her vocal and musical style, along with her level of success, has been compared to Whitney Houston and Celine Dion. Carey and her peers, according to Garry Mulholland, are "the princesses of wails [...] virtuoso vocalists who blend chart-oriented pop with mature MOR torch song".[249] Author and writer Lucy O'Brien attributed the comeback of Barbra Streisand's "old-fashioned showgirl" to Carey and Dion, and described them and Houston as "groomed, airbrushed and overblown to perfection".[249] Carey's musical transition and use of more revealing clothing during the late 1990s were, in part, initiated to distance herself from this image, and she subsequently said that most of her early work was "schmaltzy MOR".[249] Some have noted that unlike Houston and Dion, Carey co-writes her own songs, and the *Guinness Rockopedia* (1998) classified her as the "songbird supreme".[250]

Legacy

Carey at Edwards Air Force Base during the making of the "I Still Believe" video in 1998

Carey's vocal style and singing ability have significantly impacted popular and contemporary music. As music critic G. Brown from *The Denver Post* wrote, "For better or worse, Mariah Carey's five-octave range and melismatic style have influenced a generation of pop singers."[251] According to *Rolling Stone*, "Her mastery of melisma, the fluttering strings of notes that decorate songs like "Vision of Love", inspired the entire *American Idol* vocal school, for better or worse, and virtually every other female R&B singer since the Nineties."[252] Jody Rosen of *Slate Magazine* wrote of Carey's influence in modern music, calling her the most influential vocal stylist of the last two decades, the person who made rococo melismatic singing.[253] Rosen further exemplified Carey's influence by drawing parallel with American Idol, which to her, "often played out as a clash of melisma-mad Mariah wannabes. And, today, nearly 20 years after Carey's debut, major labels continue to bet the farm on young stars such as the winner of Britain's X Factor show, Leona Lewis, with her Generation Next gloss on Mariah's big voice and big hair."[253] Sean Daly of *St. Petersburg Times* wrote, "Depending on how you feel about public humiliation, the best/worst parts of American Idol are the audition shows, which normally break down into three distinct parts:(1) The Talented Kids.(2) The Weird Kids.(3) The Mariahs." Daly further commented, "The Mariahs are the hardest ones to watch, mainly because most of them think they're reeeaaally good. The poor, disillusioned hopefuls plant themselves in front of judges Simon Cowell, Paula Abdul and Randy Jackson – then proceed to stretch, break and mutilate every note of a song, often Mariah's Hero, a tune that has ruined more throats than smoker's cough."[254] *New York Magazine's* editor Roger Deckker said that in regarding Carey as an influential artist in music, he commented that "Whitney Houston may have introduced melisma (the vocally acrobatic style of lending a word an extra syllable or twenty) to the charts, but it was Mariah—with her jaw-dropping range—who made it into America's default sound."[255] Deckker also added that "Every time you turn on American Idol, you are watching her children".[255] Despite her vocal prowess, Carey's vocal technique particularly with the use of melisma and belting, has been subject to public scrutiny mainly because of young singers such as from talent shows have been overly imitating her singing technique in which critics commented "Mariah Carey is, without a doubt, the worst thing to happen to amateur singing since the karaoke machine".[254] As Professor Katherine L. Meizel noted in her book, "The Mediation of Identity Politics in American Idol", "Carey's influence not just stops in the emulation of melisma or her singing amongst the wannabe's, it's also her persona, her diva, her stardom which inspires them.... a pre-fame conic look."[256]

> The problem, however, is that for all her talent, the 36-year-old is first and foremost a STAR, the very epitome of pop opulence in today's celebrity-dependent culture. And thus, millions of young women and men wake up every morning and figure that, simply by imitating Carey's vocal derring-do, they too can wind up on the cover of People or on MTV Cribs or on the arm of record mogul Tommy Mottola.
>
> —Sean Daly from *St. Petersburg Times* commenting on Carey's popularity and influence on aspiring singers and on worldwide talent shows.[257]

Carey's influence is notable in numerous hip hop, pop and R&B artists, including Beyoncé,[62] Mary J. Blige,[258] Christina Aguilera,[259] Rihanna,[260] Kelly Clarkson,[261] Nelly Furtado,[262] Leona Lewis,[263] Brandy Norwood,[252] Jessica Simpson,[245] Pink,[264] and Missy Elliott, among others.[62] Knowles credits Carey's singing and her song "Vision of Love" as influencing her to begin practicing vocal "runs" as a child, as well as helping her pursue a career as a musician.[62] Rihanna has stated that Carey is one of her major influences and idol.[] Christina Aguilera has cited in her early stages of her career that Carey is a big influence in her singing career and being one of her idols.[259] According to Pier Dominguez, author of *Christina Aguilera: a star is made : the unauthorized biography*, Aguilera has stated how she loved listening to Whitney Houston, but it was Carey who had the biggest influence on her vocal styling. Carey's carefully choreographed image of a grown woman's image struck a chord on Aguilera. Her influence on Aguilera also grew from the fact that both were of mixed heritage.[265] Philip Brasor, editor of *The Japan Times*, expressed how Carey's vocal and melismatic style even influenced Asian singers. He wrote regarding

Japanese superstar Utada Hikaru, "Utada sang what she heard, from the diaphragm and with her own take on the kind of melisma that became de rigueur in American pop after the ascendance of Mariah Carey."[266] In an article called "Out With Mariah's Melisma, In With Kesha's Kick", writer David Browne of *The New York Times* discusses how the ubiquitous melisma pop style has suddenly fallen down from pop culture in favor of young stars who uses the now ubiquitous autotune in which the first mentioned was heavily popularized into mainstream pop culture with the likes of Mariah Carey and Whitney Houston.[267] Browne had commented "But beginning two decades ago, melisma overtook pop in a way it hadn't before. Mariah Carey's debut hit from 1990, "Vision of Love," followed two years later by Whitney Houston's version of "I Will Always Love You," set the bar insanely high for notes stretched louder, longer and knottier than most pop fans had ever heard."[267] Browne further added "A subsequent generation of singers, including Ms. Aguilera, Jennifer Hudson and Beyoncé, built their careers around melisma. (Men like Brian McKnight and Tyrese also indulged in it, but women tended to dominate the form.)"[267]

Carey is also credited for introducing R&B and hip hop into mainstream pop culture, and for popularizing rap as a featuring act through her post-1995 songs.[62] Sasha Frere-Jones, editor of *The New Yorker* commented, "It became standard for R&B/hip-hop stars like Missy Elliott and Beyoncé, to combine melodies with rapped verses. And young white pop stars—including Britney Spears, 'N Sync, and Christina Aguilera—have spent much of the past ten years making pop music that is unmistakably R&B."[62] Moreover Jones concludes that "[Carey's] idea of pairing a female songbird with the leading male MCs of hip-hop changed R&B and, eventually, all of pop. Although now anyone is free to use this idea, the success of "The Emancipation of Mimi" suggests that it still belongs to Carey."[62] Judnick Mayard, writer of *The Fader*, wrote that in regarding of R&B and hip hop collaboration, "The champion of this movement is Mariah Carey."[268] Mayard also expressed that "To this day ODB and Mariah may still be the best and most random hip hop collaboration of all time", citing that due to the record "Fantasy", "R&B and Hip Hop were the best of step siblings."[268] Kelfa Sanneh of *The New York Times* wrote, "In the mid-1990's Ms. Carey pioneered a subgenre that some people call the thug-love duet. Nowadays clean-cut pop stars are expected to collaborate with roughneck rappers, but when Ms. Carey teamed up with Ol' Dirty Bastard, of the Wu-Tang Clan, for the 1995 hit "Fantasy (Remix)", it was a surprise, and a smash."[76] Aside from her pop culture and musical influence, Carey is credited for releasing a classic Christmas song called "All I Want For Christmas Is You".[] In a retrospective look at Carey's career, Sasha Frere-Jones of *The New Yorker* said, the "charming" song was one of Carey's biggest accomplishments, calling it "one of the few worthy modern additions to the holiday canon".[62] *Rolling Stone* ranked "All I Want for Christmas Is You" fourth on its Greatest Rock and Roll Christmas Songs list, calling it a "holiday standard."[65] Following the release of her *Greatest Hits* album, Devon Powers of Popmatters has said in his review that "She has influenced countless female vocalists after her. At 32, she is already a living legend—even if she never sings another note."[269] Carey's acumen also extended for being a successful businesswoman, with the launch of her perfumes, her clothing line and books.[270] She has portrayed the true nature of being a superstar, according to sociologist Naomi Hirahara, and is a classic example of the word "diva". Carey is never seen without her large entourage, whether it be award shows, performances or as guests on late night specials. Hirahara says, "her demands are sporadic, her looks are glamorous, she is hardly of her age, but she is still ruling. Nowadays people emulate the idea of being a diva, but Carey was the original one in true sense of the term."[270]

Honors and awards

Mariah Carey during red carpet interviews at the 82nd Academy Awards

Throughout Carey's career, she has collected many honors and awards, including the World Music Awards' Best Selling Female Artist of the Millennium, the Grammy's Best New Artist in 1991, Billboard's Special Achievement Award for the Artist of the Decade during the 1990s.[271] In a career spanning over 20 years, Carey has sold over 200 million albums, singles, and videos worldwide, making her one of the biggest-selling artists in music history. Carey is ranked as the best-selling female artist of the Nielsen SoundScan era, with over 52 million copies sold.[272][273][274][275] Possessing a five-octave vocal range, Carey was ranked first in MTV and *Blender* magazine's 2003 countdown of the 22 Greatest Voices in Music, and was placed second in *Cove* magazine's list of "The 100 Outstanding Pop Vocalists".[276][236] Aside from her voice, she has become known for her songwriting. Yahoo Music editor Jason Ankeny wrote, "She earned frequent comparison to rivals Whitney Houston and Celine Dion, but did them both one better by composing all of her own material."[277] According to *Billboard* magazine, she was the most successful artist of the 1990s in the United States.[278] At the 2000 World Music Awards, Carey was given a Legend Award for being the "best-selling female pop artist of the millennium", as well as the "Best-selling artist of the 90s" in the United States, after releasing a series of albums of multi-platinum status in Asia and Europe, such as *Music Box* and *Number 1's*.[276][279] She is also a recipient of the Chopard Diamond Award in 2003, recognizing sales of over 100 million albums worldwide.[280] Additionally, the Recording Industry Association of America (RIAA) lists Carey as the third-best-selling female artist, with shipments of over 63 million units in the US.[281][282] In Japan, Carey has the top four highest-selling albums of all time by a non-Asian artist.[283][284]

Carey has spent a record 79 weeks at the number-one position on *Billboard* Hot 100, becoming the artist with the most weeks at number-one in US chart history.[285] On that same chart, she has accumulated 18 number-one singles, which ties her with Elvis Presley for the second most number-one singles in the chart's history (after only The Beatles).[286] In 1994, Carey released her holiday album *Merry Christmas* has sold over 15 million copies worldwide, and is the best-selling Christmas album of all time.[63][287][64][288] It also produced the successful single "All I Want for Christmas Is You", which became the only holiday song and ringtone to reach multi-platinum status in the US.[289] In Japan, *Number 1's* has sold over 3,250,000 copies and is the best-selling album of all time in Japan by a non-Asian artist.[290] Her hit single "One Sweet Day", which featured Boyz II Men, spent sixteen consecutive weeks at the top of *Billboard*'s Hot 100 chart in 1996, setting the record for the most weeks atop the Hot 100 chart in history.[275] After Carey's success in Asia with *Merry Christmas*, *Billboard* estimated Carey as the all-time best-selling international artist in Japan.[291] In 2008, *Billboard* listed "We Belong Together" ninth on The Billboard Hot 100 All-Time Top Songs[149] and second on Top Billboard Hot 100 R&B/Hip-Hop Songs.[292] The song was also declared the most popular song of the 2000s decade by *Billboard*.[152] In 2009, Carey's cover of Foreigner's song "I Want to Know What Love Is" became the longest-running number-one song in Brazilian singles chart history, spending 27 consecutive weeks at number-one.[293] Additionally, Carey has had three songs debut at number-one on the *Billboard* Hot 100: "Fantasy", "One Sweet Day" and "Honey", making her the artist with the most number-one debuts in the chart's 52-year history.[294] Also, she is the first female artist to debut at number 1 in the U.S. with "Fantasy".[276] In 2010, Carey's 13th album and second Christmas album, *Merry Christmas II You*, debuted at No.1 on the R&B/Hip-Hop Albums chart, making it only the second Christmas album to top that chart. On November 19, 2010, *Billboard* magazine named Carey in their "Top 50 R&B/Hip-Hop Artists of the Past 25 Years" chart at number four.[295]

Philanthropy and other activities

Carey is a philanthropist who has donated time and money to organizations such as the Fresh Air Fund.[296] She became associated with the Fund in the early 1990s, and is the co-founder of a camp located in Fishkill, New York, that enables inner-city youth to embrace the arts and introduces them to career opportunities.[296] The camp was called Camp Mariah "for her generous support and dedication to Fresh Air children", and she received a Congressional Horizon Award for her youth-related charity work.[297] She is well-known nationally for her work with the Make-A-Wish Foundation in granting the wishes of children with life-threatening illnesses, and in November 2006 she was awarded the Foundation's Wish Idol for her "extraordinary generosity and her many wish granting achievements".[298][299] Carey has volunteered for the New York City Police Athletic League and contributed to the obstetrics department of New York Presbyterian Hospital Cornell Medical Center.[300] A percentage of the sales of *MTV Unplugged* was donated to various other charities.[300] In 2008, Carey was named Hunger Ambassador of the World Hunger Relief Movement.[301] In February 2010, the song, "100%", which was originally written and recorded for the film, *Precious*,[302] was used as one of the theme songs for the 2010 Winter Olympics, with all money proceeds going to Team USA.[303]

One of Carey's most high-profile benefit concert appearances was on VH1's 1998 *Divas Live* special, during which she performed alongside other female singers in support of the Save the Music Foundation.[97] The concert was a ratings success, and Carey participated in the Divas 2000 special.[97] In 2007, the Save the Music Foundation honored Carey at their tenth gala event for her support towards the foundation since its inception.[146][304] She appeared at the *America: A Tribute to Heroes* nationally televised fundraiser in the aftermath of the September 11 attacks, and in December 2001, she performed before peacekeeping troops in Kosovo.[305] Carey hosted the CBS television special *At Home for the Holidays*, which documented real-life stories of adopted children and foster families, from the Wayback Machine on October 22, 2001.[306] In 2005, Carey performed for Live 8 in London[307] and at the Hurricane Katrina relief telethon "Shelter from the Storm".[308] In August 2008, Carey and other singers recorded the charity single, "Just Stand Up" produced by Babyface and L. A. Reid, to support "Stand Up to Cancer".[309]

Declining offers to appear in commercials in the United States during her early career, Carey was not involved in brand marketing initiatives until 2006, when she participated in endorsements for Intel Centrino personal computers and launched a jewelry and accessories line for teenagers, Glamorized, in American Claire's and Icing stores.[310] During this period, as part of a partnership with Pepsi and Motorola, Carey recorded and promoted a series of exclusive ringtones, including "Time of Your Life".[311] She signed a licensing deal with the cosmetics company Elizabeth Arden, and in 2007, she released her own fragrance, "M".[312] According to *Forbes*, Carey was the fifth richest woman in entertainment as of January 2007, with an estimated net worth of US $270 million.[313][314] In November 2011, it was reported that Carey's net worth was valued at more than $500 million.[315] On November 29, 2010, Mariah debuted a collection on HSN, the collection range included jewelry, shoes and fragrances.[316] In

November 2011, Carey was announced as the new global ambassador for Jenny Craig, following her 70-pound (**unknown operator: u'strong'** kg) weight loss with the program after giving birth to fraternal twins in April.[317]

Filmography

Year	Title	Role	Notes
1999	***The Bachelor***	Ilana	
2001	***Glitter***	Billie Frank	2001 Golden Raspberry Award for Worst Actress
2002	***WiseGirls***	Raychel	
2003	***Death of a Dynasty***	Herself	Cameo appearance
2005	***State Property 2***	Dame's Wifey	
2008	***You Don't Mess with the Zohan***	Herself	Cameo appearance
2009	***Tennessee***	Krystal	
2009	***Precious***	Mrs. Weiss	Breakthrough Performance Award at the Palm Springs International Film Festival Supporting Actress of the Year at the Capri Hollywood International Film Festival Nominated – Black Reel Award for Best Supporting Actress & Best Ensemble Nominated – NAACP Image Award for Outstanding Supporting Actress in a Motion Picture Nominated – Screen Actors Guild Award for Outstanding Cast in a Motion Picture Nominated – Critics' Choice Awards for Best Acting Ensemble

Year	Title	Role	Notes
2002	***Ally McBeal***	Candy Cushnip	"Playing with Matches" (Season 5, episode 8)
2003	***The Proud Family***	Herself	Voice role

Discography

- *Mariah Carey* (1990)
- *Emotions* (1991)
- *Music Box* (1993)
- *Merry Christmas* (1994)
- *Daydream* (1995)
- *Butterfly* (1997)
- *Rainbow* (1999)
- *Glitter* (2001)
- *Charmbracelet* (2002)
- *The Emancipation of Mimi* (2005)
- *E=MC²* (2008)
- *Memoirs of an Imperfect Angel* (2009)
- *Merry Christmas II You* (2010)

Notes

[1] Nickson 1998, pp. 8
[2] Nickson 1998, pp. 7
[3] "Mariah Carey Biography" (http://movies.nytimes.com/person/10883/Mariah-Carey). *The New York Times* (The New York Times Company). . Retrieved 2011-08-14.
[4] "Celebrity Central: Top 25 Celebrities: Mariah Carey" (http://www.people.com/people/mariah_carey). *People* (Time Warner). . Retrieved 2011-08-14.
[5] Nickson 1998, pp. 9
[6] Nickson 1998, pp. 14
[7] Nickson 1998, pp. 10–11
[8] Nickson 1998, pp. 13
[9] Nickson 1998, pp. 16
[10] Nickson 1998, pp. 17
[11] Nickson 1998, pp. 18
[12] Nickson 1998, pp. 19
[13] Nickson 1998, pp. 20
[14] Nickson 1998, pp. 21
[15] Nickson 1998, pp. 22
[16] Nickson 1998, pp. 61
[17] Nickson 1998, pp. 25
[18] Nickson 1998, pp. 26
[19] Goodman, Fred (1991-04-14). "Pop Music; The Marketing Muscle Behind Mariah Carey" (http://www.nytimes.com/1991/04/14/arts/pop-music-the-marketing-muscle-behind-mariah-carey.html). . Retrieved 2011-08-14.
[20] Italie, Hillel (1990-08-18). "Vocal Range lets Carey Soar to the Top" (http://news.google.com/newspapers?id=ivFRAAAAIBAJ&sjid=1m4DAAAAIBAJ&pg=6885,6109094&dq=mariah+carey+cinderella&hl=en). *Pittsburgh Post-Gazette* (John Robinson Block). . Retrieved 2011-08-18.
[21] Nickson 1998, pp. 25
[22] Nickson 1998, pp. 28–29
[23] Nickson 1998, pp. 33
[24] Nickson 1998, pp. 45
[25] Landis, David (1991-05-13). "'Bathgate' Wait" (http://pqasb.pqarchiver.com/USAToday/access/56149786.html?dids=56149786:56149786&FMT=ABS&FMTS=ABS:FT&type=current&date=May+13,+1991&author=David+Landis&pub=USA+TODAY+(pre-1997+Fulltext)&desc=`BATHGATE'+WAIT&pqatl=google). *USA Today* (Gannett Company). . Retrieved 2011-08-14.
[26] Bartha, Agatha (1991-02-12). "Major Grammy Winners" (http://pqasb.pqarchiver.com/thestar/access/461628961.html?FMT=ABS&FMTS=ABS:FT&type=current&date=Feb+21,+1991&author=AP&pub=Toronto+Star&desc=Major+Grammy+winners&pqatl=google). *Toronto Star* (Torstar). . Retrieved 2011-08-18.
[27] "Year Ends Well for Countries Hottest Stars" (http://pqasb.pqarchiver.com/chicagotribune/access/24482822.html?dids=24482822:24482822&FMT=ABS&FMTS=ABS:FT&type=current&date=Dec+27,+1991&author=Jan+DeKnock.&pub=Chicago+Tribune+(pre-1997+Fulltext)&desc=Year+ends+well+for+country's+hottest+stars&pqatl=google). *Chicago Tribune* (Tribune Company). 1991-12-27. . Retrieved 2011-08-19.
[28] Harrington, Richard (1992-01-01). "1991's Chart-Toppers: Garth, Mariah & CC" (http://pqasb.pqarchiver.com/washingtonpost/access/73919427.html?dids=73919427:73919427&FMT=ABS&FMTS=ABS:FT&type=current&date=Jan+01,+1992&author=Richard+Harrington&pub=The+Washington+Post+(pre-1997+Fulltext)&desc=1991's+Chart-Toppers:+Garth,+Mariah+&+CC&pqatl=google). *The Washington Post* (The Washington Post Company). . Retrieved 2011-08-19.
[29] Cane, Clay (2010-06-12). "Mariah Celebrates Twenty Years" (http://www.bet.com/news/celebrities/2010/06/11/mariahtwenty.html). *Black Entertainment Television*. Viacom. . Retrieved 2010-08-15.
[30] Nickson 1998, pp. 50–51
[31] Nickson 1998, pp. 52
[32] Nickson 1998, pp. 53
[33] Nickson 1998, pp. 58
[34] Nickson 1998, pp. 59
[35] "Mariah Carey: Emotions" (http://www.sonymusic.co.jp/Music/International/Arch/SR/MariahCarey/SICP-8076/index.html) (in Japanese). *Sony Music Entertainment Japan*. Sony. . Retrieved 2011-03-19.
[36] Shapiro 2001, pp. 68
[37] Shapiro 2001, pp. 69
[38] Nickson 1998, pp. 71
[39] Shapiro 2001, pp. 70
[40] Nickson 1998, p. 72
[41] Nickson 1998, pp. 77–78
[42] Nickson 1998, p. 79
[43] Nickson 1998, p. 80
[44] "RIAA Gold & Platinum > Mariah Carey" (http://www.riaa.com/goldandplatinumdata.php?resultpage=2&table=SEARCH_RESULTS&action=&title=&artist=mariah carey&format=ALBUM&debutLP=&category=&sex=&releaseDate=&requestNo=&type=&level=&label=&company=&certificationDate=&awardDescription=&catalogNo=&aSex=&rec_id=&charField=&gold=&platinum=&multiPlat=&level2=&certDate=&album=&id=&after=&before=&startMonth=1&endMonth=1&startYear=1958&endYear=2009&sort=Artist&perPage=25). Recording Industry Association of America. . Retrieved 2011-01-14.
[45] Williams, Chris (2011-07-03). "Mariah Carey's Music Box LP (1993) Revisited With Co-Writer Walter Afanasieff" (http://www.soulculture.co.uk/features/interviews/mariah-careys-music-box-lp-1993-revisited-with-co-writer-walter-afanasieff-return-to-the-classics/). *Soul Culture*. Soul Culture Media. . Retrieved 2011-07-14.
[46] Shapiro 2001, pp. 72–73
[47] Shapiro 2001, pp. 74
[48] Shapiro 2001, pp. 75
[49] Shapiro 2001, pp. 77
[50] Shapiro 2001, pp. 78

[51] Wynn, Ron. "Music Box > Overview" (http://www.allmusic.com/album/r186574). *Allmusic*. All Media Guide. . Retrieved 2010-08-17.
[52] Nickson 1998, p. 102
[53] "Chartverfolgung/Carey, Mariah/Single" (http://musicline.de/de/chartverfolgung_summary/artist/Carey,Mariah/single?sort=entry) (in German). musicline.de PhonoNet. . Retrieved 2010-01-21.
[54] "Search The Charts" (http://www.irishcharts.ie/search/placement). The Irish Charts. Irish Recorded Music Association. . Retrieved 2010-10-23.
[55] "Mariah Carey – Without You" (http://austriancharts.at/showitem.asp?interpret=Mariah+Carey&titel=Without+You&cat=s) (in German). *Ö3 Austria Top 40*. Hung Medien. . Retrieved 2011-08-19.
[56] Nickson 1998, p. 112
[57] Shapiro 2001, pp. 81
[58] Shapiro 2001, pp. 82
[59] Shapiro 2001, pp. 86–87
[60] Nickson 1998, p. 132
[61] Nickson 1998, p. 133
[62] Frere-Jones, Sasha (2006-04-06). "Mariah Carey's Record-Breaking Career" (http://www.newyorker.com/archive/2006/04/03/060403crmu_music). *The New Yorker* (Condé Nast Publications). . Retrieved 2011-11-10.
[63] Thompson, Tom (2008-04-19). "Let the Yuel Duel Begin" (http://www.telegraph.co.uk/culture/music/rockandjazzmusic/3648757/Let-the-yule-duel-begin.html). *The Daily Telegraph* (Telegraph Media Group). . Retrieved 2011-05-10.
[64] Hancox, Dan (2010-11-26). "Sounds of the Season" (http://www.thenational.ae/arts-culture/music/sounds-of-the-season?pageCount=0). *The National* (Mubadala Development Company). . Retrieved 2010-12-10.
[65] Greene, Andy. "The Greatest Rock and Roll Christmas Songs" (http://www.rollingstone.com/music/photos/the-greatest-rock-and-roll-christmas-songs-20101216/mariah-carey-all-i-want-for-christmas-is-you-0150435). *Rolling Stone*. Wenner Media. . Retrieved 2010-12-20.
[66] "Mariah Carey's 'All I Want For Christmas Is You' Is World's First Double Platinum Holiday Ringtone" (http://www.prnewswire.com/news-releases/mariah-careys-all-i-want-for-christmas-is-you-is-worlds-first-double-platinum-holiday-ringtone-79488972.html). Legacy Recordings. PR Newswire. . Retrieved 2010-11-10.
[67] McClure, Steve (1995-08-05). *The World's Number-Two Music Market Is No Afterthought* (http://books.google.com/books?id=xwsEAAAAMBAJ&pg=PA57&dq=mariah+carey+japanese&hl=en&ei=IvVbTOTmBcH48AbW69zlAg&sa=X&oi=book_result&ct=result&resnum=2&ved=0CCoQ6AEwAQ#v=onepage&q=mariah carey japanese&f=false). Prometheus Global Media. . Retrieved 2010-08-15.
[68] "RIAJ - Statistics - Other Data - List of Million-Certified Compact Discs by Year - 1994" (http://www.riaj.or.jp/data/others/million_list/1994.html) (in Japanese). Recording Industry Association of Japan. . Retrieved 2011-08-19.
[69] "RIAJ - Statistics - Certification of Music Download - December 2008" (http://www.riaj.or.jp/data/others/chart/w090120_3.html) (in Japanese). Recording Industry Association of Japan. . Retrieved 2011-08-19.
[70] Nickson 1998, pp. 136–137
[71] Shapiro 2001, pp. 91
[72] Shapiro 2001, pp. 89
[73] Nickson 1998, p. 145
[74] Trust, Gary (2010-06-02). "'20/20': Mariah Marks Milestone" (http://www.billboard.com/column-chartbeat/20-20-vision-mariah-marks-milestone-1004094895.story#/column-chartbeat/20-20-vision-mariah-marks-milestone-1004094895.story). *Billboard*. Prometheus Global Media. . Retrieved 2011-08-19.
[75] McClure, Steve (1996-01-27). "Carey's Ubiquitous Japanese Success" (http://books.google.com/books?id=7g4EAAAAMBAJ&pg=PA68&dq=mariah+carey+japanese&hl=en&ei=GvtbTIz9MsH-8Aazw4XYAg&sa=X&oi=book_result&ct=book-thumbnail&resnum=5&ved=0CDUQ6wEwBA#). *Billboard*. Prometheus Global Media. . Retrieved 2010-10-20.
[76] Sanneh, Kalefa (2005-08-10). "The Summer Buzz: Cicadas and Mariah Carey" (http://www.nytimes.com/2005/08/04/arts/music/04note.html?ei=5090&en=4901ecf683560cdf&ex=1280808000&partner=rssuserland&emc=rss&pagewanted). *The New York Times* (The New York Times Company). . Retrieved 2011-08-14.
[77] Nickson 1998, p. 153
[78] Speare, Aiden (1996-01-30). "Garth Brooks Refuses Trophy at American Music Awards" (http://news.google.com/newspapers?id=_JFSAAAAIBAJ&sjid=7DYNAAAAIBAJ&pg=1353,4731300&dq=mariah+carey+american+music+awards&hl=en). *The Post and Courier* (Evening Post Publishing Company). . Retrieved 2011-08-19.
[79] Shapiro 2001, pp. 95
[80] Shapiro 2001, pp. 96
[81] McClure, Steve (1996-12-28). "The Year in Japan" (http://books.google.com/books?id=sQkEAAAAMBAJ&lpg=PA1&pg=PA62#v=onepage&q&f=false). *Billboard*. Prometheus Global Media. . Retrieved 2011-08-19.
[82] Sischy, Ingrid (2007-09-20). "Mariah Carey: The Naked Truth From The World's Biggest Diva". *Interview*. pp. 156–165.
[83] Nickson 1998, p. 156
[84] Nickson 1998, p. 164
[85] Nickson 1998, p. 157
[86] Nickson 1998, pp. 158–159
[87] Tainen, Dave (1997-09-16). "Carey' 'Butterfly' Shows but Thin" (http://news.google.com/newspapers?id=YzkdAAAAIBAJ&sjid=MC4EAAAAIBAJ&pg=6616,590422&dq=mariah+carey+breathy+voice&hl=en). *Milwaukee Journal Sentinel* (Journal Communications). . Retrieved 2011-08-19.
[88] Demone, Larry (1997-03-07). "In Brief" (http://nl.newsbank.com/nl-search/we/Archives?p_product=BN&p_theme=bn&p_action=search&p_maxdocs=200&p_topdoc=1&p_text_direct-0=0EAF9A6859F16A45&p_field_direct-0=document_id&p_perpage=10&p_sort=YMD_date:D&s_trackval=GooglePM). *The Buffalo News* (Berkshire Hathaway). . Retrieved 2011-08-05.
[89] Juzwiak, Rich (2005-04-15). "Mariah Carey - Butterly" (http://www.slantmagazine.com/music/review/mariah-carey-butterfly/330). Slant Magazine. . Retrieved 2010-12-20.
[90] Shapiro 2001, pp. 104
[91] Shapiro 2001, pp. 101
[92] Friedman, Roger (2008-04-03). "Mariah Carey's Biography" (http://www.foxnews.com/story/0,2933,205054,00.html). Fox News. News Corporation. . Retrieved 2011-08-06.
[93] Shapiro 2001, pp. 102
[94] Hoskyns, Barney (1997-12-12). "Mariah Carey - Butterfly" (http://www.rollingstone.com/music/albumreviews/butterfly-19971030). *Rolling Stone*. Wenner Media. . Retrieved 2011-08-19.

[95] Erlewine, Stephen Thomas (2008-04-12). "(((Butterfly > Overview)))" (http://www.allmusic.com/album/r314312/review). *Allmusic*. Rovi Corporation. . Retrieved 2011-08-09.
[96] Shapiro 2001, pp. 114
[97] Haring, Bruce (1998-04-16). "VH! Display of Divas Makes Me Feel 'Natural'" (http://pqasb.pqarchiver.com/USAToday/access/28692993.html?dids=28692993:28692993&FMT=ABS&FMTS=ABS:FT&type=current&date=Apr+16,+1998&author=Bruce+Haring&pub=USA+TODAY&desc=VH1+display+of+'Divas'+makes+all+feel+'Natural'&pqatl=google). *USA Today* (Gannet Company). . Retrieved 2011-08-19.
[98] Rodman, Sarah (2001-09-11). "All That Litters, 'Glitter'" (http://pqasb.pqarchiver.com/bostonherald/access/80313960.html?dids=80313960:80313960&FMT=ABS&FMTS=ABS:FT&type=current&date=Sep+11,+2001&author=SARAH+RODMAN&pub=Boston+Herald&desc=Music;+All+that+litters+`Glitter';+Carey+displays+newfound+maturity+-+when+you+can+hear+her+among+the+guest+stars&pqatl=google). *Boston Herald* (Herald Media Inc.). . Retrieved 2011-02-05.
[99] Shapiro 2001, pp. 115
[100] Shapiro 2001, pp. 116
[101] Willis, Andrew (1998-11-18). "Higher and Higher" (http://books.google.com/books?id=jisEAAAAMBAJ&pg=PA96&lpg=PA96&dq=Everybody+swung+it+like+I+didn't+want+to+put+something+out+because+I+wouldn't+accept+less+than+a+number+1+pop+single.+That's+not+even+true.+Like+I+didn't+want+to+'break+a+streak'&source=bl&ots=MLJyxyQfpM&sig=pQyEle8DiX5QDTlw1SE1g4GjpxY&hl=en&ei=LbqiTLO2NYGB8gaRqJzZCg&sa=X&oi=book_result&ct=result&resnum=2&ved=0CBcQ6AEwAQ#v=onepage&q=Everybody swung it like I didn't want to put something out because I wouldn't accept less than a number 1 pop single.That's not even true.Like I didn't want to 'break a streak'&f=false). *Vibe*. InterMedia Partners. . Retrieved 2011-08-14.
[102] Vineyard, Jennifer (1998-08-31). "Mariah Talks About Whitney Duet, Takes Stage With Jermaine Dupri And Da Brat" (http://www.mtv.com/news/articles/1426947/19980831/carey_mariah.jhtml). *MTV*. Viacom. . Retrieved 2010-09-29.
[103] Doughrey (1998-12-14). "Mariah and Whitney Team Up!" (http://books.google.co.kr/books?id=GcQDAAAAMBAJ&pg=PA60&dq=Mariah+and+I+got+along+very+great.+We+had+never+talked+and+never+sang+together+before.+We+just+had+a+chance+for+camaraderie,+singer-to-singer,+artist-to-artist,+that+kind+of+thing.+We+just+laughed+and+talked+and+laughed+and+talked+and+sang+in+between+that+...+It's+good+to+know+that+two+ladies+of+soul+can+still+be+friends."&hl=ko&ei=NIZNTsfZJ8acgQeLvczyBg&sa=X&oi=book_result&ct=result&resnum=1&ved=0CCsQ6AEwAA#v=onepage&q=Mariah and I got along very great.We had never talked and never sang together before.We just had a chance for camaraderie, singer-to-singer, artist-to-artist, that kind of thing.We just laughed and talked and laughed and talked and sang in between that ...It's good to know that two ladies of soul can still be friends."&f=false). *Ebony*. Johnson Publishing Company. . Retrieved 2011-08-19.
[104] McClure, Steve (1999-01-23). "International News" (http://books.google.co.kr/books?id=yg0EAAAAMBAJ&pg=PA49&dq=bodyguard+top+foreign+album&lr=&as_brr=0&as_pt=MAGAZINES&cd=5#v=onepage&q=bodyguard top foreign album&f=false). *Billboard*. Prometheus Global Media. . Retrieved 2010-10-03.
[105] Nickson 1998, p. 153
[106] "Live Nation – Mariah Carey: #1's" (http://www.store.livenation.com/Product.aspx?cp=13281_25619_25593_25883_29557&pc=MUDD548). *Live Nation*. Live Nation Entertainment. . Retrieved 2010-08-24.
[107] Shapiro 2001, pp. 121
[108] Shapiro 2001, pp. 122
[109] Shapiro 2001, pp. 123
[110] Shapiro 2001, pp. 133
[111] Shapiro 2001, pp. 134
[112] Shapiro 2001, pp. 135
[113] Graeme, Virtue (1999-11-07). "Rainbow: Mariah Carey (Columbia)" (http://pqasb.pqarchiver.com/smgpubs/access/70150818.html?dids=70150818:70150818&FMT=ABS&FMTS=ABS:FT&type=current&date=Nov+07,+1999&author=Graeme+Virtue&pub=Sunday+Herald&desc=Rainbow+Mariah+Carey+(Columbia)+HHH&pqatl=google). *Sunday Herald* (Newsquest). . Retrieved 2011-08-19.
[114] Linden, Amy (1999-12-12). "Mariah Carey 'Rainbow'" (http://books.google.com/books?id=YCgEAAAAMBAJ&pg=PA260-IA6&dq=mariah+carey+rainbow&hl=en&ei=qyduTabsD8G4tgfdvezwDg&sa=X&oi=book_result&ct=result&resnum=5&ved=0CEQQ6AEwBA#v=onepage&q=mariah carey rainbow&f=false). *Vibe*. InterMedia Partners. . Retrieved 2011-03-06.
[115] "Winners of the World Music Awards" (http://web.archive.org/web/20001015144058/www.montecarloresort.com/awards/00/w00res00.htm). *World Music Awards*. Société des bains de mer de Monaco. . Retrieved August 18, 2010.
[116] "EMI Drops Mariah Carey" (http://news.bbc.co.uk/2/hi/entertainment/1777172.stm). *BBC News*. BBC. 2002-01-31. . Retrieved 2011-02-03.
[117] Erlewine, Stephen Thomas. "(((Glitter > Overview)))" (http://allmusic.com/album/glitter-r544381). *Allmusic*. Rovi Corporation. . Retrieved 2011-02-21.
[118] Friedman, Roger (2001-07-26). "Mariah Melts Down; Madonna Disappoints" (http://www.foxnews.com/story/0,2933,30577,00.html). *Fox News*. Fox News Channel. . Retrieved 2011-08-19.
[119] Davies, Hugh (2001-07-28). "Let Me Sort Myself Out, Singer Carey Tells Fans" (http://www.telegraph.co.uk/news/main.jhtml?xml=/news/2001/07/28/wcarey28.xml). *The Daily Telegraph* (Telegraph Media Group). . Retrieved 2011-08-19.
[120] Gardner, Elysa (2002-11-28). "Mariah Carey, 'Standing Again'" (http://www.usatoday.com/life/dcovfri.htm). *USA Today* (Gannett Company). . Retrieved 2011-08-19.
[121] Pareles, Jon (2002-01-22). "Record Label Pays Dearly To Dismiss Mariah Carey" (http://www.nytimes.com/2002/01/24/us/record-label-pays-dearly-to-dismiss-mariah-carey.html). *The New York Times* (The New York Times Company). . Retrieved 2011-02-05.
[122] Vineyard, Jennifer (2005-10-13). "Mariah Carey Hospitalized For 'Extreme Exhaustion'" (http://www.mtv.com/news/articles/1445424/mariah-carey-hospitalized.jhtml). *MTV News*. Viacom. . Retrieved 2011-03-29.
[123] Vineyard, Jennifer (2005-10-13). "Mariah Carey Had 'Breakdown,' Her Publicist Says" (http://www.mtv.com/news/articles/1445918/mariah-carey-had-breakdown.jhtml). *MTV News*. Viacom. . Retrieved 2011-03-29.
[124] Gardner, Elysa (2001-09-09). "Mystery Shadows Carey's Career, Pressures Linger After Singer's Breakdown" (http://pqasb.pqarchiver.com/USAToday/access/77238866.html?dids=77238866:77238866&FMT=ABS&FMTS=ABS:FT&type=current&date=Aug+09,+2001&author=Elysa+Gardner+and+Kelly+Carter&pub=USA+TODAY&desc=Mystery+shadows+Carey's+career+Pressures+linger+after+singer's+breakdown&pqatl=google). *USA Today* (Gannett Company). . Retrieved 2011-06-16.
[125] Hiatt, Brian (2005-10-13). "Mariah Carey Had 'Breakdown,' Her Publicist Says" (http://www.mtv.com/news/articles/1445918/mariah-carey-had-breakdown.jhtml). *MTV News*. Viacom. . Retrieved 2011-03-29.
[126] Hutchinson, Bill (2001-09-11). "Delay May Dull Carey's 'Glitter'" (http://articles.nydailynews.com/2001-08-07/news/18353379_1_pop-diva-mariah-carey-delayed-movie). *Daily News* (Mortimer Zuckerman). . Retrieved 2011-02-05.
[127] Reynolds, Simon (2010-01-26). "Carey Blames 9/11 For 'Glitter' Flop" (http://www.digitalspy.com/movies/news/a199302/carey-blames-911-for-glitter-flop.html). *Digital Spy*. Hachette Filipacchi Médias. . Retrieved 2011-04-13.

[128] Patterson, Sylvia (2000-03-17). "Mariah Carey: Come in and Smell the Perfume" (http://www.telegraph.co.uk/arts/main.jhtml?xml=/arts/2008/03/16/sv_mariahcarey.xml). *The Daily Telegraph* (Telegraph Media Group). . Retrieved 2011-08-19.
[129] Johnson, Kevin C. (2001-09-16). "Mariah Carey's 'Glitter' is a Far Cry from Golden" (http://nl.newsbank.com/nl-search/we/Archives?p_product=SL&p_theme=sl&p_action=search&p_maxdocs=200&p_topdoc=1&p_text_direct-0=0EF07AA04681F07C&p_field_direct-0=document_id&p_perpage=10&p_sort=YMD_date:D&s_trackval=GooglePM). *St. Louis Post-Dispatch* (Lee Enterprises). . Retrieved 2011-08-19.
[130] Zwecker, Bill (2002-01-22). "Mariah Carries On With Record Deal, Recovery" (http://nl.newsbank.com/nl-search/we/Archives?p_product=CSTB&p_theme=cstb&p_action=search&p_maxdocs=200&p_topdoc=1&p_text_direct-0=0F115C6D597A4809&p_field_direct-0=document_id&p_perpage=10&p_sort=YMD_date:D&s_trackval=GooglePM). *Chicago Sun-Times* (Sun-Times Media Group). . Retrieved 2011-06-16.
[131] Adams, Josh (2006-02-06). "The Fall and Rise of Mariah Carey" (http://news.bbc.co.uk/1/hi/entertainment/4690602.stm). *BBC News*. BBC. . Retrieved 2011-08-19.
[132] Holson, Lisa (2002-02-21). "Mariah Carey And Universal Agree to Terms Of Record Deal" (http://query.nytimes.com/gst/fullpage.html?res=9E04E5D71330F93AA35756C0A9649C8B63). *The New York Times* (The New York Times Company). . Retrieved 2011-08-19.
[133] Dotson, Rader (2005-05-05). "I Didn't Feel Worthy Of Happiness" (http://www.parade.com/articles/editions/2005/edition_06-05-2005/featured_0). *Parade* (American Media, Inc.). . Retrieved 2011-08-19.
[134] Friedman, Roger (2002-01-14). "Mariah Makes Good in Mob Movie" (http://www.foxnews.com/story/0,2933,42928,00.html). *Fox News*. Fox News Channel. . Retrieved 2011-08-19.
[135] Willis, George (2002-02-05). "Safe To Say, Super Bowl Was One Major Success" (http://pqasb.pqarchiver.com/nypost/access/105343986.html?dids=105343986:105343986&FMT=ABS&FMTS=ABS:FT&type=current&date=Feb+05,+2002&author=George+Willis&pub=New+York+Post&desc=SAFE+TO+SAY,+SUPER+BOWL+WAS+ONE+MAJOR+SUCCESS&pqatl=google). *New York Post* (News Corporation). . Retrieved 2011-08-19.
[136] Anderman, Joan (2003-09-10). "For Carey, the Glory's Gone but the Glitter Lives On" (http://pqasb.pqarchiver.com/boston/access/403302181.html?FMT=ABS&FMTS=ABS:FT&type=current&date=Sep+10,+2003&author=Joan+Anderman,+Globe+Staff&pub=Boston+Globe&desc=FOR+CAREY,+THE+GLORY'S+GONE+BUT+THE+GLITTER+LIVES+ON&pqatl=google). *The Boston Globe* (The New York Times Company). . Retrieved 2011-08-19.
[137] Erlewine, Stephen Thomas (2002-12-03). "(((Charmbracelet > Overview)))" (http://www.allmusic.com/album/charmbracelet-r617273/review). *Allmusic*. Rovi Corporation. . Retrieved 2011-06-13.
[138] Patel, Joseph. "Carey Maps Out 'Intimate Evening' Tour" (http://www.vh1.com/news/articles/1472736/20030616/index.jhtml). *VH1*. MTV Networks (Viacom). . Retrieved 2011-06-15.
[139] Patel, Joseph. "Mariah Carey Scraps Arena Tour, Opts To Get More Intimate" (http://www.vh1.com/news/articles/1471917/mariah-carey-scraps-arena-tour.jhtml). *VH1*. Viacom. . Retrieved 2011-06-15.
[140] "Mariah's Malaysia Concert Ill-timed, Says Muslim Leader" (http://nl.newsbank.com/nl-search/we/Archives?p_product=SJ&s_site=mercurynews&p_multi=SJ&p_theme=realcities&p_action=search&p_maxdocs=200&p_topdoc=1&p_text_direct-0=1002404456D02378&p_field_direct-0=document_id&p_perpage=10&p_sort=YMD_date:D&s_trackval=GooglePM). *San Jose Mercury News*. MediaNews Group. 2004-01-16. . Retrieved 2011-06-15.
[141] "Mariah Adds UK To World Tour" (http://news.bbc.co.uk/2/hi/entertainment/2932336.stm). *BBC News*. BBC. 2003-05-31. . Retrieved 2011-02-03.
[142] Asilo, Rito P. (2003-11-23). "Mariah Carey Thrills Euphoric Manila Crowd" (http://news.google.com/newspapers?id=9LhjAAAAIBAJ&sjid=eyUMAAAAIBAJ&pg=1866,15841802&dq=mariah+carey+manila&hl=en). *Philippine Daily Inquirer*. Philippine Daily Inquirer, Inc.. . Retrieved 2011-06-13.
[143] Ehrlich, Dimitri (2005-05-05). "Revolutions" (http://books.google.com/books?id=FCcEAAAAMBAJ&pg=PA139&dq=mariah+carey+say+something&hl=en&ei=5ixOTZOyJsOblgfHiOjzDw&sa=X&oi=book_result&ct=result&resnum=1&ved=0CCcQ6AEwAA#v=onepage&q=mariah carey say something&f=false). *Vibe*. InterMedia Partners. . Retrieved 2011-02-05.
[144] Sullivan, Caroline (2005-04-01). "Mariah Carey, The Emancipation of Mimi" (http://www.guardian.co.uk/music/2005/apr/01/popandrock.shopping2). *The Guardian* (Guardian Media Group). . Retrieved 2011-08-19.
[145] Gardner, Elysa (2005-04-13). "Mariah Rebounds, Garbage is Sweet, Will Smith Gets Lost" (http://www.usatoday.com/life/music/reviews/2005-04-11-listen-up_x.htm). *USA Today* (Gannett Company). . Retrieved 2011-08-19.
[146] "Jermaine Dupri Wins R&B Song Grammy; Virgin Urban Music President Dupri Shares Songwriting Honors With Mariah Carey and So So Def/Virgin Artist Johnta Austin" (http://business.highbeam.com/436102/article-1G1-141877770/jermaine-dupri-wins-rb-song-grammy-virgin-urban-music). Business Wire. Berkshire Hathaway. 2006-04-16. . Retrieved 2011-08-19.
[147] Cinquemani, Sal (2005-04-05). "Mariah Carey: The Emancipation Of Mimi" (http://www.slantmagazine.com/music/review/mariah-carey-the-emancipation-of-mimi/560). Slant Magazine. . Retrieved 2011-08-19.
[148] Pietroluongo, Silvio (2005-09-24). "The Billboard Hot 100" (http://books.google.com/books?id=sBMEAAAAMBAJ&pg=PA75&dq=we+belong+together+review+billboard&hl=en&ei=hPgvTsroB4-2tgf6qMCjCQ&sa=X&oi=book_result&ct=result&resnum=3&ved=0CDEQ6AEwAg#v=onepage&q&f=false). *Billboard*. Prometheus Global Media. . Retrieved 2011-09-27.
[149] "The Billboard Hot 100 All-Time Top Songs (10-01)" (http://www.billboard.com/specials/hot100/charts/top100-titles-10.shtml). *Billboard*. Prometheus Global Media. 2010-09-24. . Retrieved 2011-09-27.
[150] Trust, Gary (2010-06-25). "Ask Billboard: Katy Perry, Christina Aguilera, Lady Gaga" (http://www.billboard.com/column/ask-billboard-katy-perry-christina-aguilera-1004100889.story#/column/ask-billboard-katy-perry-christina-aguilera-1004100889.story). *Billboard*. Prometheus Global Media. . Retrieved 2011-08-18.
[151] "2005 Year End Charts – Hot 100 Songs" (http://www.billboard.biz/bbbiz/charts/yearendcharts/2005/hsititl.jsp). *Billboard*. Nielsen Business Media, Inc. 2005-11-05. . Retrieved 2011-07-27.
[152] "The Billboard Hot 100 Singles & Tracks – Decade Year End Charts" (http://www.billboard.biz/bbbiz/charts/decadeendcharts/2009/hot100-songs). *Billboard*. Prometheus Global Media. . Retrieved 2011-08-19.
[153] Gundersen, Edna (2005-12-08). "Carey, West, Legend Lead The Grammy pack" (http://www.usatoday.com/life/music/awards/grammys/2005-12-08-grammy-nominations_x.htm?loc=interstitialskip). *USA Today* (Gannett Company). . Retrieved 2011-08-19.
[154] Susman, Gary (2005-12-29). "Mariah Carey Has the Year's Top-selling CD" (http://popwatch.ew.com/2005/12/29/sorry_fiddy_mar/). *Entertainment Weekly*. Time Warner. . Retrieved 2011-08-19.
[155] "Top 50 Global Best Selling Albums for 2005" (http://www.musikindustrie.de/uploads/media/top50-2005.pdf). Bundesverband Musikindustrie. . Retrieved 2011-08-19.
[156] "Coldplay Top 2005's Global Charts" (http://news.bbc.co.uk/2/hi/entertainment/4865716.stm). *BBC News*. BBC. 2006-03-31. . Retrieved 2011-08-19.
[157] "Coldplay Tops Worldwide Sales for 2005" (http://www.cbc.ca/arts/story/2006/03/31/musicsales-coldplay.html). *CBC News*. Canadian Broadcasting Corporation. 2006-03-31. . Retrieved 2011-08-19.

[158] Thompson, Ben (2008-04-19). "Pop CDs of the week: Mariah Carey, Pete Molinari and more..." (http://www.telegraph.co.uk/culture/3672721/Pop-CDs-of-the-week-Mariah-Carey-Pete-Molinari-and-more....html). *The Daily Telegraph* (Telegraph Media Group). . Retrieved 2011-08-19.
[159] Rayner, Ben (2005-12-09). "Mariah Carey, Meet U2, Kelly; Comeback Stalled as U2 Takes five Grammys Canadians Come Up Empty-handed at Awards Show" (http://pqasb.pqarchiver.com/thestar/access/983834771.html?FMT=ABS&FMTS=ABS:FT&type=current&date=Feb+09,+2006&author=Ben+Rayner&pub=Toronto+Star&desc=Mariah+Carey,+meet+U2,+Kelly;+Comeback+stalled+as+U2+takes+five+Grammys+Canadians+come+up+empty-handed+at+awards+show&pqatl=google). *Toronto Star* (Torstar). . Retrieved May 12, 2011.
[160] Popkin, Helen (2006-06-06). "Mariah Carey Takes on Madonna with New Tour" (http://msnbc.msn.com/id/14190642/site/todayshow/ns/today-entertainment/t/mariah-carey-takes-madonna-new-tour/). *MSNBC*. NBCUniversal. . Retrieved 2011-08-19.
[161] Vineyard, Jennifer (2006-05-22). "Mariah Carey Plots Mimi's Touring Adventure" (http://www.mtv.com/news/articles/1532213/mariah-carey-plots-mimis-touring-adventure.jhtml). *MTV News*. Viacom. . Retrieved 2011-08-18.
[162] Dratler, David (2006-05-26). "Carey, Jackson Spice Up Old Hits" (http://news.google.com/newspapers?id=s3A0AAAAIBAJ&sjid=5ccEAAAAIBAJ&pg=4671,3521347&dq=mariah+carey+the+adventures+of+mimi&hl=en). *TimesDaily* (Tennessee Valley Printing Co., Inc.). . Retrieved 2011-08-18.
[163] Roura, Phil (2005-12-30). "Carey Set for August" (http://articles.nydailynews.com/2006-06-02/entertainment/18330712_1_lobster-chefs-coney-island). *Daily News* (Mortimer Zuckerman). . Retrieved 2011-08-18.
[164] Badershall, Jami (2006-05-25). "Mimi Taps 'Idol' Judge" (http://news.google.com/newspapers?id=PEguAAAAIBAJ&sjid=eGQFAAAAIBAJ&pg=1508,4685271&dq=mariah+carey+the+adventures+of+mimi&hl=en). *Sun Journal* (Sun Media). . Retrieved 2011-08-18.
[165] Vineyard, Jennifer (2006-08-30). "Mariah Carey Tour Kickoff: The Voice Outshines Costume Changes, Video Clips" (http://www.mtv.com/news/articles/1537972/mariah-carey-tour-kickoff-all-about-voice.jhtml). *MTV News*. Viacom. . Retrieved 2011-08-18.
[166] Rafer, Guzman (2006-09-10). "Mimi Hits the Garden, Just Like That" (http://pqasb.pqarchiver.com/newsday/access/1105356491.html?dids=1105356491:1105356491&FMT=ABS&FMTS=ABS:FT&type=current&date=Aug+24,+2006&author=RAFER+GUZMN.+STAFF+WRITER&pub=Newsday+(Combined+editions)&desc=Mimi+hits+the+Garden,+just+like+that&pqatl=google). *Newsday* (Cablevision). . Retrieved 2011-08-18.
[167] "'Comeback' Succeeded For Carey In Tunis" (http://mariahcarey.com/news/15321). Mariahcarey.com. 2006-07-22. . Retrieved 2011-08-18.
[168] "Mariah Carey's Hong Kong Concert Called Off" (http://www.foxnews.com/story/0,2933,225444,00.html). *Fox News*. News Corporation. 2006-10-10. .
[169] Flaminger, Michael (2006-10-30). "People" (http://www.nytimes.com/2006/10/30/style/30iht-peeptue.3332215.html). *The New York Times* (The New York Times Company). . Retrieved 2011-08-18.
[170] Ryan, Joyal (2006-08-29). "Mariah Sues, Tries to Aid Mongolians" (http://www.eonline.com/uberblog/b53741_Mariah_Sues_Tries_to_Aid_Mongolians_.html). *E!*. NBCUniversal. . Retrieved 2011-08-18.
[171] Starr, Michael (2008-04-19). "Yes On Dubya Apology Frost" (http://www.nypost.com/p/pagesix/cindy_adams/item_QYji9hBaJmhBk7ito9jshO;jsessionid=3036AFA318523D15C26D85EFEFAC2961). *New York Post* (News Corporation). . Retrieved 2011-05-10.
[172] Bulgram, Angela (2008-04-18). "Mariah Reveals 'E=MC' Album Title Meaning" (http://www.nme.com/news/mariah-carey/35852). *NME*. IPC Media. . Retrieved 2011-08-09.
[173] Macpherson, Alex (2008-04-16). "Mariah Carey: E=MC²" (http://www.guardian.co.uk/music/2008/apr/11/popandrock.alexispetridis). *The Guardian* (Guardian Media Group). . Retrieved 2011-08-05.
[174] Richard, David (2008-04-08). "CD: Mariah Carey's 'E=MC2'" (http://www.latimes.com/entertainment/news/music/la-et-mariah12apr12,1,6445816.story). *Los Angeles Times* (Tribune Company). . Retrieved 2011-08-09.
[175] Guthrie, Marisa (2008-04-04). "Elvis is Spotted - Rolling in His Grave" (http://today.msnbc.msn.com/id/23918924/ns/today-entertainment/t/mariah-carey-surpasses-elvis-no-s/). *Daily News* (Mortimer Zuckerman). . Retrieved 2011-08-06.
[176] "Mariah Breaks Elvis Chart Record" (http://news.bbc.co.uk/2/hi/entertainment/7327843.stm). *BBC News*. BBC. 2008-04-04. . Retrieved 2011-08-06.
[177] "Billboard Hot 100 Chart 50th Anniversary" (http://www.billboard.com/bbcom/specials/hot100/charts/top100-artists-20.shtml). *Billboard*. Prometheus Global Media. . Retrieved 2011-08-19.
[178] McKay, Hollie (2008-04-03). "Mariah Carey, Nick Cannon Get Wedding Tattoos" (http://www.foxnews.com/story/0,2933,354539,00.html). *Fox News*. News Corporation. . Retrieved 2011-08-06.
[179] Vineyard, Jennier (2008-04-09). "It's Official! Mariah Carey, Nick Cannon Wedding Photo, Comments Are Released" (http://www.mtv.com/news/articles/1586974/mariah-carey-nick-cannon-wedding-photo-released.jhtml). *MTV News*. Viacom. . Retrieved 2011-05-10.
[180] Danner, Sarah (2008-03-30). "'Am I Pregnant? We'll See...' Says Mariah Carey in Revealing Interview" (http://www.dailymail.co.uk/tvshowbiz/article-1092935/Am-I-pregnant-Well--says-Mariah-Carey-revealing-interview.html). *Daily Mail* (Daily Mail and General Trust). . Retrieved 2011-08-06.
[181] Pareles, Jon (2009-01-22). "Music Review; Music for Many Firsts, Including the First Couple's First Dance" (http://query.nytimes.com/gst/fullpage.html?res=9F03E5DD1F3FF931A15752C0A96F9C8B63). *The New York Times* (The New York Times Company). . Retrieved 2011-08-19.
[182] Dubozinskis, Alex (2009-07-06). "Mariah Carey Among Jackson Memorial Participants" (http://www.reuters.com/article/2009/07/06/us-jackson-idUSTRE5615KN20090706). *Reuters*. The Thomson Corporation. . Retrieved 2011-08-19.
[183] Vena, Jocelyn (2009-07-08). "Mariah Carey Worries She 'Let Everybody Down' At Jackson Memorial" (http://www.mtv.com/news/articles/1615530/mariah-carey-reflects-on-jackson-memorial.jhtml). *MTV News*. Viacom. . Retrieved 2011-08-19.
[184] O'Niel, Tom (2009-10-19). "Dark horse nominees: Will the Oscars nominate 'Avatar'?" (http://goldderby.latimes.com/awards_goldderby/2009/10/avatar-james-cameron-movie-news-story-article.html). *Los Angeles Times* (Tribune Company). . Retrieved 2011-08-19.
[185] Anderson, John (2009-01-18). "Precious: Based on the Novel 'Push' by Sapphire Movie Review From The Sundance Film Festival" (http://www.timeout.com/film/reviews/87257/precious-based-on-the-novel-push-by-sapphire.html?cpage=2&ccat=11). *Variety*. Reed Business Information. . Retrieved 2011-08-19.
[186] "Entertainment; Precious Film Takes Sundance Prize" (http://news.bbc.co.uk/2/hi/entertainment/8265281.stm). *BBC News*. BBC. 2009-09-20. . Retrieved 2011-08-19.
[187] "Movies – News – 'Precious' Scoops Top Toronto Prize" (http://www.digitalspy.com/movies/a178373/precious-scoops-top-toronto-prize.html). *Digital Spy*. Hachette Filipacchi Médias. 2009-09-21. . Retrieved 2011-08-19.
[188] "Weeks After Tipsy Awards Speech, Mariah Carey Pops Cork on her Own Liquor Brand, Angel Champagne" (http://www.nydailynews.com/gossip/2010/01/16/2010-01-16_mariah_launches_new_liquor_label.html). *Daily News* (Mortimer Zuckerman). 2010-01-17. . Retrieved 2011-08-19.

[189] Erlewine, Stephen Thomas (2009-09-29). "Memoirs of an Imperfect Angel > Review" (http://www.allmusic.com/album/r1616570/review). *Allmusic*. Rovi Corporation. . Retrieved 2011-08-19.
[190] "New CDs" (http://www.nytimes.com/2009/09/28/arts/music/28choi.html?_r=1). *The New York Times* (The New York Times Company). 2009-09-29. . Retrieved 2011-08-19.
[191] Up for Discussion Jump to Forums (2009-09-29). "Barbra Streisand Surprises With Ninth No. 1 On Billboard 200" (http://www.billboard.com/news/barbra-streisand-surprises-with-ninth-no-1004019217.story). *Billboard*. Prometheus Global Media. . Retrieved 2011-08-19.
[192] Ben-Yehuda, Ayala (2009-07-16). "Mariah Carey Hit The Billboard Hot 100" (http://www.billboard.com/#/news/hannah-montana-mariah-carey-hit-the-billboard-1003994566.story). *Billboard*. Prometheus Global Media. . Retrieved 2009-08-16.
[193] Martens, Todd (2009-09-30). "Mariah Carey: Are We Obsessed?" (http://latimesblogs.latimes.com/music_blog/2009/06/mariah-carey-are-we-obsessed.html). *Los Angeles Times* (Tribune Company). . Retrieved 2011-08-14.
[194] Reid, Shaheem (2009-06-30). "Is Mariah Carey's 'Obsessed' Directed At Eminem?" (http://www.mtv.com/news/articles/1614088/mariah-careys-obsessed-directed-at-eminem.jhtml). *MTV News*. Viacom. . Retrieved 2011-08-13.
[195] "Mariah Carey Does It Big In Brazil" (http://www.rap-up.com/2010/08/22/mariah-carey-does-it-big-in-brazil/). *Rap-Up*. Devin Lazerine. . Retrieved 2011-08-19.
[196] Martin, Devin (2010 01-30). "Mariah Carey Announces 'Angels Advocate' Release Date" (http://www.independent.co.uk/arts-entertainment/music/news/mariah-carey-announces-angels-advocate-release-date-1884367.html). *The Independent* (Alexander Lebedev). .
[197] "Mariah Carey Falls On Stage" (http://www.digitalspy.com/music/news/a278887/mariah-carey-falls-on-stage.html). *Digital Spy*. Hachette Filipacchi Médias. 2009-09-21. . Retrieved 2011-08-19.
[198] Dubozinskis, Alex (2009-07-06). "Maraih Carey Remix Album Delayed to March 30" (http://www.reuters.com/article/2009/07/06/us-jackson-idUSTRE5615KN20090706). *Reuters*. The Thomson Corporation. . Retrieved 2011-08-19.
[199] Vozick, Simon (2010-03-23). "Mariah Carey: 'Angels Advocate' Remix Album Cancelled" (http://music-mix.ew.com/2010/03/23/mariah-carey-angels-advocate-cancelled/). *Entertainment Weekly*. Time Warner. . Retrieved 2011-08-19.
[200] "Mariah's Album Ditched" (http://www.mtv.com.au/news/a4d4fa76-vh1-mariahs-album-ditched/). *MTV Australia*. Viacom. 2010-03-22. . Retrieved 2011-08-19.
[201] "J.D. Talks New Mariah Carey Album" (http://www.rap-up.com/2010/05/05/jd-talks-new-mariah-carey-album/). *Rap-Up*. Devin Lazerine. . Retrieved 2011-08-19.
[202] "Mariah Carey Touches Down in Brazil" (http://www.rap-up.com/2010/08/19/mariah-carey-touches-down-in-brazil/). *Rap-Up*. Devin Lazerine. 2010-08-19. . Retrieved 2011-08-19.
[203] Bakker, Tiffany (2010-09-10). "Get Ready for a Very Carey Christmas" (http://www.heraldsun.com.au/ipad/get-ready-for-a-very-carey-christmas/story-fn6bn9st-1225962016819). *Herald Sun* (The Herald and Weekly Times). . Retrieved 2011-08-19.
[204] "Exclusive: Mariah Carey Christmas Album Title, Release Date Revealed" (http://www.rap-up.com/2010/09/01/exclusive-mariah-carey-christmas-album-title-release-date-revealed/). *Rap-Up*. Devin Lazerine. . Retrieved 2011-08-19.
[205] Caulfield, Keith (2010-11-10). "Country Albums Rule Top Three on Billboard 200" (http://www.billboard.com/news/country-albums-rule-top-three-on-billboard-1004125997.story?tag=hpfeed). *Billboard*. Prometheus Global Media. . Retrieved 2011-08-19.
[206] Ramirez, Rauly (2010-12-10). "R&B/Hip-Hop Chart Juice: Kanye West, Nicki Minaj and Ne-Yo" (http://www.billboard.com/news/r-b-hip-hop-chart-juice-kanye-west-nicki-1004133614.story#/news/r-b-hip-hop-chart-juice-kanye-west-nicki-1004133614.story). *Billboard*. Prometheus Global Media. . Retrieved 2011-08-19.
[207] Green, Anna (2010-05-29). "Mariah Carey Drops Out of Film Due to Medical Reasons" (http://articles.nydailynews.com/2010-05-28/gossip/27065557_1_fuels-rumors-imperfect-angel-social-worker). *Daily News* (Mortimer Zuckerman). . Retrieved 2011-08-19.
[208] Herrera, Monica (2008-11-28). "Mariah Carey Confirms: I'm Pregnant" (http://www.billboard.com/news/mariah-carey-confirms-i-m-pregnant-1004124338.story#/news/mariah-carey-confirms-i-m-pregnant-1004124338.story). *Billboard*. Prometheus Global Media. . Retrieved 2011-08-09.
[209] Derschowitz, Jessica (2008-11-24). "Mariah Carey: I'm Pregnant" (http://www.cbsnews.com/8301-31749_162-20021007-10391698.html). *CBS News*. CBS. . Retrieved 2011-08-09.
[210] "Mariah Carey & Nick Cannon Welcome Twins" (http://www.eonline.com/uberblog/b239514_mariah_carey_nick_cannon_welcome_twins.html). *E! Entertainment Television*. NBCUniversal. 2011-04-30. . Retrieved 2011-08-19.
[211] Quan, Denise. "Mariah Carey and Nick Cannon Reveal Baby Names" (http://marquee.blogs.cnn.com/2011/05/04/mariah-carey-and-nick-cannon-reveal-baby-names/). *CNN*. Turner Broadcasting System. .
[212] Corner, Lewis (2001-08-02). "Amy Winehouse, Lady GaGa on Tony Bennett's 'Duets II' Tracklisting" (http://www.digitalspy.com/music/news/a332887/amy-winehouse-lady-gaga-on-tony-bennetts-duets-ii-tracklisting.html). *Digital Spy*. Hachette Filipacchi Médias. . Retrieved 2011-08-19.
[213] Lipshutz, Jason (2011-05-13). "Nick Cannon, Mariah Carey, Working on New Album" (http://www.billboard.com/column/the-juice/nick-cannon-mariah-carey-working-on-new-1005182852.story#/column/the-juice/nick-cannon-mariah-carey-working-on-new-1005182852.story). *Billboard*. Prometheus Global Media. . Retrieved 2011-08-19.
[214] Perricone, Kathleen (2011-05-16). "Mariah Carey Planning to Release Album this Year" (http://www.nydailynews.com/entertainment/music/2011/05/15/2011-05-15_mariah_carey_planning_to_release_a_new_album_this_year_singer_recorded_it_while_.html). *Daily News*. Mortimer Zuckerman. . Retrieved 2011-08-19.
[215] Vena, Jocelyn (2011-10-05). "Justin Bieber Confirms Mariah Carey Christmas Collabo" (http://www.mtv.com/news/articles/1672005/justin-bieber-christmas-mariah-carey.jhtml). *MTV News*. MTV. . Retrieved 2011-11-10.
[216] "Mariah Carey Remakes Christmas Classic With Mariah Carey" (http://www.rap-up.com/2011/10/04/mariah-carey-remakes-christmas-classic-with-justin-bieber/). *Rap-Up*. Devin Lazerine. . Retrieved 2011-08-19.
[217] "Mariah Carey and Justin Bieber Shut Down Macy's" (http://www.rap-up.com/2011/11/05/mariah-carey-and-justin-bieber-shut-down-macys-for-christmas-video/). *Rap-Up*. Devin Lazarine. . Retrieved 2011-11-11.
[218] "Exclusive: Mariah Carey on Marriage, Miscarriage and Motherhood" (http://abcnews.go.com/blogs/entertainment/2011/10/exclusive-mariah-carey-on-marriage-miscarriage-and-motherhood/). ABC News. The Walt Disney Company. 2011-10-28. . Retrieved 2011-11-11.
[219] "Mariah Carey Guests On Uncle Murda's 'Warning'" (http://www.rap-up.com/2011/10/31/new-music-uncle-murda-f-mariah-carey-50-cent-young-jeezy-warning-remix/). *Rap-Up*. Devin Lazarine. . Retrieved 2011-11-11.
[220] "Mariah Carey and John Legend Duet on 'When Christmas Comes'" (http://www.rap-up.com/2011/11/09/mariah-carey-and-john-legend-to-throw-house-party-in-christmas-video/). *Rap-Up*. Devin Lazarine. . Retrieved 2011-11-11.
[221] Farley, Christopher John. "Pop's Princess Grows Up" (http://www.time.com/time/archive/preview/0,10987,134725,00.html). *Time* (Time Warner). . Retrieved 2011-08-19.

[222] "More Like a Screaming 'Mimi'" (http://articles.nydailynews.com/2005-04-12/entertainment/18289697_1_voice-cover-singing). *Daily News* (Mortimer Zuckerman). 2005-04-15. . Retrieved 2011-08-19.
[223] Berger, Arion (1991-08-10). "Mariah Carey: 'Emotions'" (http://www.ew.com/ew/article/0,,20272922,00.html). *Entertainment Weekly*. Time Warner. . Retrieved 2011-08-19.
[224] Walters, Barry (2001-09-04). "Marked Woman" (http://www.villagevoice.com/2001-09-04/music/marked-woman/). *The Village Voice* (Village Voice Media). . Retrieved 2011-09-18.
[225] Sawey, Evan (2008-05-01). "Mariah Carey: E=MC² < Reviews" (http://www.popmatters.com/pm/review/mariah-carey-emc2). PopMatters. . Retrieved 2010-02-10.
[226] Hoard, Christian (2008-02-28). "Mariah's E=MC2: A First Listen to Carey's Eleventh Studio Album" (http://www.rollingstone.com/music/news/mariahs-e-mc2-a-first-listen-to-careys-eleventh-studio-album-20080228). *Rolling Stone*. Wenner Media. . Retrieved 2011-08-08.
[227] Norris, John (2003-10-20). "Mariah: Remixes, Reunions and Russia". *MTV*. Viacom.
[228] "100 Greatest Dance Songs: 100–91" (http://web.archive.org/web/20060820164653/http://www.slantmagazine.com/iframes/dance_100/100_91.asp). Slant Magazine. 2006-04-25. . Retrieved 2011-08-19.
[229] Cinquemani, Sal (2005-11-11). "Gem Carey" (http://www.ew.com/ew/article/0,,1048283,00.html). *Entertainment Weekly*. Time Warner. . Retrieved 2011-08-19.
[230] Willis, Andrew (1998-11-18). "Cinderella Stroy" (http://books.google.com/books?id=Wy0EAAAAMBAJ&pg=PA57&dq=knows+the+importance+of+mixes,+so+you+feel+like+you're+with+an+artist+who+appreciates+your+workâan+artist+who+wants+to+come+up+with+something+with+you&hl=en&ei=0oRPTs6aJMm1twfZkpGpBw&sa=X&oi=book_result&ct=result&resnum=1&ved=0CCoQ6AEwAA#v=onepage&q=knows the importance of mixes, so you feel like you're with an artist who appreciates your workâan artist who wants to come up with something with you&f=false). *Vibe*. InterMedia Partners. . Retrieved 2011-08-14.
[231] "Roll Over Elvis - Mariah is Here" (http://nl.newsbank.com/nl-search/we/Archives?p_product=PI&s_site=philly&p_multi=PI&p_theme=realcities&p_action=search&p_maxdocs=200&p_topdoc=1&p_text_direct-0=10EC2F88C5EE2870&p_field_direct-0=document_id&p_perpage=10&p_sort=YMD_date:D&s_trackval=GooglePM). *The Philadelphia Inquirer* (Philadelphia Media Holdings). 2008-03-20. . Retrieved 2011-08-19.
[232] Anderson, Joan (2006-02-06). "Carey, On!" (http://pqasb.pqarchiver.com/boston/access/983024561.html?FMT=ABS&FMTS=ABS:FT&type=current&date=Feb+05,+2006&author=Joan+Anderman,+GLOBE+STAFF&pub=Boston+Globe&desc=CAREY,+ON!&pqatl=google). *The Boston Globe* (The New York Times Company). . Retrieved 2011-08-19.
[233] Harris, James (1990-08-28). "Her 7-Octave Voice Finally Gets Noticed" (http://pqasb.pqarchiver.com/orlandosentinel/access/90254402.html?dids=90254402:90254402&FMT=ABS&FMTS=ABS:FT&type=current&date=Aug+28,+1990&author=&pub=Orlando+Sentinel&desc=HER+7-OCTAVE+VOICE+FINALLY+GETS+NOTICED&pqatl=google). *Orlando Sentinel* (Tribune Company). . Retrieved 2011-08-10.
[234] Robins, Wayne (1990-08-12). "Columbia's New 'Franchise'" (http://pqasb.pqarchiver.com/newsday/access/77383942.html?dids=77383942:77383942&FMT=ABS&FMTS=ABS:FT&type=current&date=Aug+12,+1990&author=Wayne+Robins&pub=Newsday+(Combined+editions)&desc=Columbia's+New+`Franchise'&pqatl=google). *Newsday* (Cablevision). .
[235] Oleman, Sarah (2003-04-01). "Princess Positive is Taking Care of Inner Mariah" (http://www.smh.com.au/articles/2003/03/31/1048962696862.html). *The Sydney Morning Herald* (Fairfax Media). . Retrieved 2011-08-10.
[236] "100 Outstanding Pop Vocalists" (http://celebrities-group.popsugar.com/100-Outstanding-Pop-Vocalists-1659579). *Cove*. Cove Media Company. 2008-05-24. . Retrieved 2011-08-19.
[237] Viros 2009, p. 83
[238] Peckham 2005, p. 117
[239] Appleman 1986, p. 434
[240] Nickson 1998, p. 108
[241] Martin 1986, p. 9
[242] Pareles, Jon (1993-12-13). "Review/Pop; Venturing Outside the Studio, Mariah Carey Proves Her Mettle" (http://www.nytimes.com/1993/12/13/arts/review-pop-venturing-outside-the-studio-mariah-carey-proves-her-mettle.html). *The New York Times* (The New York Times Company). . Retrieved 2011-08-19.
[243] Givens, Ron (1991-08-09). "Vision of Loveliness" (http://www.ew.com/ew/article/0,,317869,00.html). *Entertainment Weekly* (Time Warner). . Retrieved 2011-08-19.
[244] Levell, Tim (2002-12-02). "Carey Charm Offensive" (http://news.bbc.co.uk/2/hi/entertainment/2535321.stm). *BBC News*. BBC. . Retrieved 2011-08-19.
[245] Gardner, Elysa (2002-12-22). "Carey Sounds Like 'Gold' on 'Charmbracelet'" (http://www.usatoday.com/life/music/reviews/2002-12-02-charmbracelet_x.htm). *USA Today* (Gannet Company). . Retrieved 2011-08-03.
[246] Morettini 2006, p. 44
[247] Norent, Lynn (1991-03-12). "Not Another White Girl Trying to Sing Black" (http://books.google.com/books?id=xcwDAAAAMBAJ&pg=PA54&dq=Mariah+Carey:+'Not+another+White+girl+trying+to+sing+Black&hl=en&ei=AZZPTpG9Do6CtgfGnNSsBw&sa=X&oi=book_result&ct=result&resnum=1&ved=0CCoQ6AEwAA#v=onepage&q=Mariah Carey: 'Not another White girl trying to sing Black&f=false). *Ebony*. Johnson Publishing. . Retrieved 2011-08-19.
[248] Shapiro 2001, p. 124
[249] Mulholland 2009, p. 57
[250] James 1998, p. 74
[251] Brown, G. (2003-08-23). "Careyed away the singer with fantastic vocal range belts out songs with technical precision and too little feeling" (http://pqasb.pqarchiver.com/sun_sentinel/access/390123241.html?dids=390123241:390123241&FMT=ABS&FMTS=ABS:FT&type=current&date=Aug+29,+2003&author=G.+Brown++The+Denver+Post&pub=South+Florida+Sun+-+Sentinel&desc=CAREYED+AWAY+THE+SINGER+WITH+THE+FANTASTIC+VOCAL+RANGE+BELTS+OUT+SONGS+WITH+TECHNICAL+PRECISION+AND+TOO+LITTLE+FEELING.&pqatl=google). *The Denver Post* (MediaNews Group). . Retrieved 2011-10-31.
[252] "100 Greatest Singers of All Time – Mariah Carey" (http://www.rollingstone.com/music/lists/100-greatest-singers-of-all-time-19691231/mariah-carey-19691231). *Rolling Stone*. Wenner Media. . Retrieved 2011-10-31.
[253] Rosen, Jody (2008-04-13). "Why The Haters Are Wrong About Mariah Carey" (http://www.slate.com/id/2190184/). *Slate*. The Washington Post Company. . Retrieved 2011-10-31.
[254] Katzif, Michael. "How 'American Idol' Uses (and Abuses) Melisma" (http://www.npr.org/templates/story/story.php?storyId=6791133). NPR Music. . Retrieved 2011-11-10.
[255] "The Most Influential People in Music" (http://nymag.com/news/features/influentials/16905/). *New York*. New York Media. 2006-05-07. . Retrieved 2011-10-31.
[256] Katherine L. Meizel, 2002, p. 83

[257] Daly, Sean (2006-10-03). "You're No Mariah!" (http://www.sptimes.com/2006/08/03/Weekend/You_re_no_Mariah.shtml). *St. Petersburg Times* (Times Publishing Company). . Retrieved 2011-10-31.
[258] "Mariah Carey - Blige Thanks 'Beautiful' Carey" (http://www.contactmusic.com/news-article/blige-thanks-beautiful-carey). Contactmusic.com. 2005-12-22. . Retrieved 2011-10-31.
[259] Catlin, Roger (2000-08-31). "A Matter of Time Christina Aguilera Says She'll Leave The Pack" (http://pqasb.pqarchiver.com/courant/access/59339487.html?dids=59339487:59339487&FMT=ABS&FMTS=ABS:FT&type=current&date=Aug+31,+2000&author=ROGER+CATLIN;+Courant+Rock+Critic&pub=Hartford+Courant&desc=A+MATTER+OF+TIME+CHRISTIANA+AGUILERA+SAYS+SHE'LL+LEAVE+THE+PACK,+INCLUDING+BRITNEY+SPEARS+IN+THE+DUST&pqatl=google). *Hartford Courant* (Tribune Company). . Retrieved 2011-07-21.
[260] Tecson, Brandee (2005-10-31). "Rihanna Brings On Acting Career With New 'Bring It On' Flick" (http://www.mtv.com/news/articles/1512953/rihanna-brings-on-acting-career-with-bring-it-on.jhtml). *MTV News*. MTV. . Retrieved 2011-11-10.
[261] "American Idol - Mariah Carey Overwhelms Kelly Clarkson" (http://www.contactmusic.com/new/xmlfeed.nsf/story/mariah-carey-overwhelms-kelly-clarkson). Contactmusic.com. 2003-07-23. . Retrieved 2011-11-10.
[262] "The Juice Is 'Loose'" (http://www.billboard.com/news/the-juice-is-loose-1002690079.story#/news/the-juice-is-loose-1002690079.story). *Billboard*. Prometheus Global Media. . Retrieved 2011-11-10.
[263] Gallo, Phil (2008-07-08). "Mariah Carey & Leona Lewis" (http://www.variety.com/article/VR1117989833?refCatId=3193). *Variety* (Reed Business Information). . Retrieved 2011-11-10.
[264] Browne, David (2010-12-24). "Trilling Songbirds Clip Their Wings" (http://www.nytimes.com/2010/12/26/arts/music/26browne.html). *The New York Times* (The New York Times Company). . Retrieved 2011-11-10.
[265] Dominguez, Pier (2003). *Christina Aguilera: a star is made : the unauthorized biography*. Amber Books Publishing. p. 134. ISBN 0-9702224-5-9.
[266] "The Naughties Played It Nice" (http://search.japantimes.co.jp/cgi-bin/fm20091218a1.html). *The Japan Times*. The Japan Times Company. 2009-12-18. . Retrieved 2011-11-10.
[267] Browne, David (2010-08-10). "Out With Mariah's Melisma, In With Kesha's Kick" (http://www.nytimes.com/2010/12/26/arts/music/26browne.html?ref=ladygaga). *The New York Times* (The New York Times Company). . Retrieved 2011-11-10.
[268] Mayard, Judnick (2009-01-04). "Suite903: R&B, Rejected and Betrayed" (http://www.thefader.com/2011/01/14/suite903-rb-rejected-and-betrayed/). The Fader. . Retrieved 2011-11-10.
[269] Powers, Devon (2002-05-08). "Mariah Carey: Greatest Hits" (http://www.popmatters.com/pm/review/careymariah-greatest). PopMatters. . Retrieved 2011-10-11.
[270] Hirahara, 2002, p. 84
[271] "Mariah Carey Career Achievement Awards" (http://mariahcarey.com/news/awards.php). Mariahcarey.com. . Retrieved 2010-09-29.
[272] "Mariah Carey Announces She Is Pregnant" (http://ca.reuters.com/article/entertainmentNews/idCATRE69R2ZD20101028). *Reuters*. Thomson Reuters. 2010-10-28. . Retrieved 2011-07-10.
[273] Teeman, Tim (2010-12-21). "'Child' Diva Mariah Carey Dances To Her Own Tune" (http://www.theaustralian.com.au/news/arts/child-diva-mariah-carey-dances-to-her-own-tune/story-e6frg8n6-1225974077690). *The Australian* (News Limited). . Retrieved 2011-07-10.
[274] Levine, Nick (2009-11-12). "Mariah Carey" (http://www.digitalspy.com/celebrities/mariah-carey/). *Digital Spy*. Hachette Filipacchi Médias. . Retrieved 2011-05-01.
[275] Up for Discussion Jump to Forums. "Billboard Magazine – 20–20 Vision Mariah Marks Milestone" (http://www.billboard.com/column-chartbeat/20-20-vision-mariah-marks-milestone-1004094895.story). *Billboard*. Prometheus Global Media. . Retrieved 2011-11-10.
[276] "Mariah Carey Biography & Awards" (http://www.billboard.com/artist/mariah-carey/bio/48340). *Billboard*. Prometheus Global Media. . Retrieved 2011-11-10.
[277] Ankeny, Jason. "Yahoo Music – Biography – Mariah Carey" (http://new.music.yahoo.com/mariah-carey/biography/). Yahoo Music. Yahoo. . Retrieved 2011-11-10.
[278] Shapiro 2001, p. 145
[279] "Monte Carlo Resort – Awards" (http://web.archive.org/web/20001015144058/www.montecarloresort.com/awards/00/w00res00.htm). World Music Awards. 2000-10-15. . Retrieved 2010-10-30.
[280] "NME Artists – Mariah Carey" (http://www.nme.com/artists/mariah-carey). *NME*. IPC Media. . Retrieved 2010-08-19.
[281] "Gold and Platinum – Top Selling Artists" (http://www.riaa.com/goldandplatinumdata.php?table=tblTopArt). Recording Industry Association of America. . Retrieved 2010-08-18.
[282] "Mariah Marks Milestone" (http://www.mariahcarey.com/news/news.php?uid=2882). MariahCarey.com. . Retrieved May 29, 2010.
[283] Nickson 1998
[284] "Carey's Ubiquitous Japanese Success" (http://books.google.com/books?id=7g4EAAAAMBAJ&lpg=PA1&pg=PA68#v=onepage&q&f=false). *Billboard*. Prometheus Global Media. 1996-01-26. . Retrieved 2011-11-10.
[285] Up for Discussion Jump to Forums. "The Emancipation of Mimi – Mariah Carey" (http://www.billboard.com/album/mariah-carey/emancipation-of-mimi/668708). *Billboard*. Prometheus Global Media. . Retrieved 2011-11-10.
[286] Hiscock, John (2009-12-10). "Mariah Carey Interview for Precious" (http://www.telegraph.co.uk/culture/film/6771071/Mariah-Carey-interview-for-Precious.html). *The Daily Telegraph* (Telegraph Media Group). . Retrieved 2011-11-10.
[287] Frere-Jones, Sasha (2006-04-03). "On Top: Mariah Carey's Record-Breaking Career" (http://www.newyorker.com/archive/2006/04/03/060403crmu_music). *The New Yorker* (Condé Nast Publications). . Retrieved 2010-12-10.
[288] "Old Chestnuts Roasting: Ghosts of Christmas Music Past" (http://www.independent.co.uk/arts-entertainment/music/features/old-chestnuts-roasting-ghosts-of-christmas-music-past-764334.html). *The Independent* (Alexander Lebedev). 2007-12-11. . Retrieved 2010-12-10.
[289] By PR Newswire (December 17, 2009). "Mariah Carey's 'All I Want For Christmas Is You' Is World's First Double Platinum Holiday Ringtone" (http://www.thestreet.com/story/10648016/mariah-careys-all-i-want-for-christmas-is-you-is-worlds-first-double-platinum-holiday-ringtone.html). TheStreet. . Retrieved June 29, 2010.
[290] *'#1's'* (http://books.google.co.kr/books?id=yg0EAAAAMBAJ&pg=PA49&dq=bodyguard+top+foreign+album&lr=&as_brr=0&as_pt=MAGAZINES&cd=5#v=onepage&q=bodyguard top foreign album&f=false). Prometheus Global Media. 1999-01-23. . Retrieved 2011-11-11.
[291] Lichtman, Irv (1994-11-26). *Mariah Hits Big n Japan* (http://books.google.com/books?id=aggEAAAAMBAJ&pg=PA136&dq=mariah+carey+merry+christmas+debut&hl=en&ei=C8p5TPW5GMOblgeMn5zsCw&sa=X&oi=book_result&ct=result&resnum=2&ved=0CDQQ6AEwAQ#v=onepage&q=mariah carey merry christmas debut&f=false). Prometheus Global Media. . Retrieved 2011-11-11.
[292] "Sweet Soul Music: Top Billboard Hot 100 R&B/Hip-Hop Songs" (http://www.billboard.com/specials/hot100/charts/top-rbhiphop.shtml). *Billboard*. Prometheus Global Media. August 15, 2010. . Retrieved August 29, 2010.
[293] "Mariah Makes Brazilian Chart History" (http://www.mariahcarey.com/news/news.php?uid=2852). Mariahcarey.com. . Retrieved 2011-11-11.

[294] "Billboard Hot 100 No. 1 Debuts" (http://www.billboard.com/slideshow/457789?decorator=slideshow&confirm=true). *Billboard*. Prometheus Global Media. . Retrieved 2010-10-10.
[295] "The Top 50 R&B / Hip-Hop Artists of the Past 25 Years" (http://www.billboard.com/#/column/the-juice/the-top-50-r-b-hip-hop-artists-of-the-past-1004127916.story?). *Billboard*. Prometheus Global Media. 2010-11-10. . Retrieved 2011-11-11.
[296] Hopkins, Eugene (1994-12-04). "Carey a Fresh Face for Fresh Air Fund" (http://news.google.com/newspapers?id=c98gAAAAIBAJ&sjid=I2sFAAAAIBAJ&pg=2220,934579&dq=camp+mariah&hl=en). *Sun Journal* (Sun Media Group). . Retrieved 2011-08-19.
[297] Vineyard, Jennifer (1999-04-13). "Mariah Carey to Receive Congressional Award for Charity Efforts" (http://www.mtv.com/news/articles/1426935/19990413/carey_mariah.jhtml). *MTV News*. Viacom. . Retrieved 2011-08-19.
[298] "Mariah Carey - Carey Packs Times Square With Early Morning Show" (http://www.contactmusic.com/news-article/carey-packs-times-square-with-early-morning-show). Contactmusic.com. 2005-04-12. . Retrieved 2011-08-19.
[299] Dinh, James (2010-12-12). "Mariah Carey Performs With Mother On Holiday TV Special" (http://www.mtv.com/news/articles/1654204/mariah-carey-performs-with-mother-on-holiday-tv-special.jhtml). Viacom. . Retrieved 2011-08-19.
[300] Snow, Shauna (2000-01-15). "Morning Reports" (http://pqasb.pqarchiver.com/latimes/access/47992976.html?dids=47992976:47992976&FMT=ABS&FMTS=ABS:FT&type=current&date=Jan+15,+2000&author=SHAUNA+SNOW&pub=Los+Angeles+Times&desc=Morning+Report;+ARTS+AND+ENTERTAINMENT+REPORTS+FROM+THE+TIMES,+NEWS+SERVICES+AND+THE+NATION'S+PRESS.&pqatl=google). *Los Angeles Times* (Tribune Company). . Retrieved 2011-08-19.
[301] Ryan, Joyal (2006-08-29). "Carey Saves the World, One Chalupa At a Time" (http://www.eonline.com/news/mariah_saves_world_one_chalupa_time/30720). *E!*. NBCUniversal. . Retrieved 2011-08-18.
[302] Kennedy, Gerrick (2010-02-26). "Mariah Carey Will Release Duet, Remix Album" (http://latimesblogs.latimes.com/music_blog/2010/02/mariah-carey-to-release-duet-remix-album.html). *Los Angeles Times* (Tribune Company). . Retrieved 2011-08-19.
[303] "AT&T to Produce Exclusive Soundtrack for Athletes Competing in 2010 Olympic Winter Game" (http://www.att.com/gen/press-room?pid=4800&cdvn=news&newsarticleid=30499). AT&T. 2010-02-26. . Retrieved 2011-08-19.
[304] Pennington, Gail (2008-04-12). "Critic's Picks" (http://nl.newsbank.com/nl-search/we/Archives?p_product=SL&p_theme=sl&p_action=search&p_maxdocs=200&p_topdoc=1&p_text_direct-0=10B0D48CAD9B00C8&p_field_direct-0=document_id&p_perpage=10&p_sort=YMD_date:D&s_trackval=GooglePM). *St. Louis Post-Dispatch* (Lee Enterprises). . Retrieved 2011-08-19.
[305] Schumacher-Rasmussen, Eric (2001-09-22). "Mariah Carey, Springsteen, Other Stars Sing For America On Telethon" (http://www.mtv.com/news/articles/1449077/carey-others-sing-on-telethon.jhtml). *MTV News*. Viacom. . Retrieved 2011-04-13.
[306] Bianculli, David (2001-12-20). "Flawed Gala On Adoption" (http://articles.nydailynews.com/2001-12-20/entertainment/18370230_1_adoption-sings-performers). *Daily News*. Mortimer Zuckerman. . Retrieved 2011-05-10.
[307] "Live 8 attracts 9.6m UK viewers" (http://news.bbc.co.uk/2/hi/entertainment/4648051.stm). *BBC News*. BBC. 2005-07-04. . Retrieved 2011-08-19.
[308] Rodman, Sarah (2005-09-10). "Stars Shine Spotlight on Needy During Katrina Relief Telethon" (http://pqasb.pqarchiver.com/bostonherald/access/894426211.html?dids=894426211:894426211&FMT=ABS&FMTS=ABS:FT&type=current&date=Sep+10,+2005&author=Sarah+Rodman&pub=Boston+Herald&desc=TELEVISION;+Stars+shine+spotlight+on+needy+during+Katrina+relief+telethon&pqatl=google). *Boston Herald* (*Herald Media Inc.*). . Retrieved 2011-08-19.
[309] Serena (2008-05-03). "Mariah, Beyoncé Top Fifth Annual Fashion Rocks" (http://www.people.com/people/article/0,,1077026,00.html). *People*. Time Warner. . Retrieved 2011-08-07.
[310] Paoletta, Michael. "The Branding of Mimi" (http://www.azcentral.com/ent/music/articles/0711mimi.html). *Billboard*. Prometheus Global Media. . Retrieved 2011-08-19.
[311] Serpe, Gina (2006-08-29). "Mariah Rings Up Pepsi" (http://www.eonline.com/uberblog/b52141_mariah_rings_up_pepsi.html). *E!*. NBCUniversal. . Retrieved 2011-08-10.
[312] Vineyard, Jennifer (2006-04-06). "Mariah Wants All Fans To See Her — And Even Smell Like Her" (http://www.mtv.com/news/articles/1528037/mariah-wants-fans-see-her-smell-like-her.jhtml). *MTV News*. Viacom. . Retrieved 2011-06-13.
[313] Thompson, Tom (2008-04-19). "The Diva has Landed" (http://www.dailytelegraph.com.au/entertainment/music/the-diva-has-landed/story-e6frexl9-1111115979296). *The Daily Telegraph* (Telegraph Media Group). . Retrieved 2011-05-10.
[314] "The Richest 20 Women In Entertainment" (http://www.forbes.com/2007/01/17/richest-women-entertainment-tech-media-cz_lg_richwomen07_0118womenstars_slide_7.html?thisSpeed=30000). *Forbes*. Forbes Publishing. 2007-01-07. . Retrieved 2011-07-10.
[315] Anderson, Kyle (2011-11-02). "Mariah Carey and Nick Cannon Let Barbara Walters Ogle Their Babies on '20/20'" (http://popwatch.ew.com/2011/10/22/mariah-carey-nick-cannon-babies-2020/). *Entertainment Weekly*. Time Warner. . Retrieved 2011-11-11.
[316] "Mariah Carey; Mariah Carey Jewelry, Shoes and Fragrances" (http://www.hsn.com/mariah-carey/mariah-carey_c-mc_a-7718_xc.aspx?rid=1831&prev=hp). *HSN*. HSN Inc.. 2011-03-03. . Retrieved 2011-08-19.
[317] Danner, Sarah (2008-03-30). "Snug as a Bug In a Rug! Mariah's 'Dembabies' Moroccan and Monroe Look Comfy and Cosy in Their Carriers" (http://www.dailymail.co.uk/tvshowbiz/article-2059911/Mariah-Carey-twins-Moroccan-Monroe-look-comfy-cosy-carriers.html?ito=feeds-newsxml). *Daily Mail* (Daily Mail and General Trust). . Retrieved 2011-08-06.

References

- Appleman, Chris (1986). *The Science of Vocal Pedagogy: Theory and Application*. Bloomington: Indiana University Press. ISBN 978-0253351103.
- James, Harold (1998). *Guinness Rockopedia*. Los Angeles: Guinness Publishing Ltd. ISBN 978-0-85112-072-5.
- Nickson, Chris (1995). *Mariah Carey: her story*. New York: St. Martin's Griffin. ISBN 978-0-312-13121-0.
- Nickson, Chris (1998). *Mariah Carey revisited*. New York: St. Martin's Griffin. ISBN 978-0-312-19512-0.
- Peckham, Anne (2005). *Vocal Workouts for the Contemporary Singer*. Boston: Berklee Press. ISBN 978-0876390475.
- Shapiro, Marc (2001). *Mariah Carey: the unauthorized biography*. Toronto: ECW Press. ISBN 978-1-5502-2444-3.
- Viros, Alexandre (2009). *Casser les Voix*. Paris: St. Martin's Griffin. ISBN 978-0-312-19512-0.
- Hardy, Phil. *The Faber Companion to 20th Century Popular Music: Fully Revised Third Edition* (2001). pg. 156–157. UK: Faber and Faber Limited. ISBN 0-571-19608-X.
- Mulholland, Garry. *The Illustrated Encyclopedia of Music* (2003). pg. 57. UK: Flame Tree Publishing. ISBN 1-904041-70-1.

- *Fred Bronson's Billboard Book of Number 1 Hits, 5th Edition* (ISBN 0-8230-7677-6)
- *Joel Whitburn Presents the Billboard Hot 100 Charts: The Sixties* (ISBN 0-89820-074-1)
- *Joel Whitburn Presents the Billboard Hot 100 Charts: The Nineties* (ISBN 0-89820-137-3)
- Additional information concerning Carey's chart history can be retrieved and verified in *Billboard's* online archive services (http://www.billboard.biz/) and print editions of the magazine.

External links

- Official website (http://www.mariahcarey.com/)
- Mariah Carey (http://www.allmusic.com/artist/p62404) at Allmusic
- Mariah Carey (http://www.imdb.com/name/nm0001014/) at the Internet Movie Database
- Mariah Carey (http://music.yahoo.com/ar-296399---Mariah-Carey) at LAUNCHcast

Ntozake Shange

Ntozake Shange	
Born	Paulette L. Williams October 18, 1948 Trenton, New Jersey
Residence	Brooklyn
Nationality	American
Alma mater	Barnard College University of Southern California
Occupation	Playwright, Author
Known for	For Colored Girls Who Have Considered Suicide When the Rainbow Is Enuf
Home town	Trenton, New Jersey
Parents	Paul T. Williams, Eloise Williams

Ntozake Shange born October 18, 1948, is an American playwright, and poet.[1] As a self proclaimed black feminist, much of the content of her work addresses issues relating to race and feminism.

Shange is best known for the Obie Award-winning play *For Colored Girls Who Have Considered Suicide When the Rainbow Is Enuf.*

She also wrote *Betsey Brown*, a novel about an African American girl who runs away from home. Among her honors and awards are fellowships from the Guggenheim Foundation and the Lila Wallace-Reader's Digest Fund, and a Pushcart Prize. Shange lives in Brooklyn.[2]

Early life

Shange was born **Paulette L. Williams**[3] in Trenton, New Jersey[4] to an upper-middle-class family. Her father, Paul T. Williams, was an Air Force surgeon, and her mother, Eloise Williams, was an educator and a psychiatric social worker. When she was 8, Shange's family moved to the racially segregated city of St. Louis. As a result of the Brown v. Board of Education court decision, Shange was bused to a white school where she endured racism and racist attacks.

Shange's family had a strong interest in the arts and encouraged her artistic education. Among the guests at their home were Dizzy Gillespie, Miles Davis, Chuck Berry, and W. E. B. Du Bois.

When Shange was 13, she returned to New Jersey, where she completed high school. In 1966 Shange enrolled at Barnard College. She graduated cum laude in American Studies, then earned a master's degree in the same field from the University of Southern California in Los Angeles. However, Shange's college years were not all pleasant. She married during her first year in college, but the marriage did not last long. Depressed over her separation and with a strong sense of bitterness and alienation, Shange attempted suicide.[5] In 1971, having come to terms with her depression and alienation, Shange changed her name. *Ntozakhe* means *she who has her own things* (literally *things that belong to her* in Xhosa) and *shange* means *he/she who walks/lives with lions* (meaning *the lion's Pride* in Zulu).[4]

Career

In 1975, Shange moved to New York City, where in that year her first and most well-known play was produced—*For Colored Girls Who Have Considered Suicide When the Rainbow is Enuf.* First produced Off-Broadway, the play soon moved on to Broadway at the Booth Theater and won a number of awards, including the Obie Award, Outer Critics Circle Award, and the AUDELCO Award. This play, her most famous work, was a 20-part poem that chronicled the lives of Black women in the United States. The poem was eventually made into the stage play, was then published in book form in 1977, then made into a movie in 2010 (*For Colored Girls*, directed by Tyler Perry). Since then, Shange has written a number of successful plays, including an adaptation of Bertolt Brecht's *Mother Courage and Her Children* (1980), which won an Obie Award.

In 2003, Shange wrote and oversaw the production of *Lavender Lizards and Lilac Landmines: Layla's Dream* while serving as a visiting artist at the University of Florida, Gainesville.

Individual poems, essays, and short stories of hers have appeared in numerous magazines and anthologies, including *The Black Scholar*, *Yardbird*, *MS*, *Essence Magazine*, *The Chicago Tribune*, *VIBE*, and *Third-World Women.*[6]

Awards

- NDEA fellow, 1973
- Obie Award
- Outer Critics Circle Award
- Audience Development Committee (Audelco) Award
- Mademoiselle Award
- Frank Silvera Writers' Workshop Award, 1978
- Los Angeles Times Book Prize for Poetry, 1981 (for *Three Pieces*)
- Guggenheim fellowship, 1981
- Medal of Excellence, Columbia University, 1981
- Obie Award, 1981, for Mother Courage and Her Children
- Nori Eboraci Award
- Barnard College, 1988
- Lila Wallace-Reader's Digest Fund annual writer's award, 1992
- Paul Robeson Achievement Award, 1992
- Arts and Cultural Achievement Award
- National Coalition of 100 Black Women (Pennsylvania chapter), 1992
- Taos World Poetry Heavyweight Champion, 1992, 1993, 1994
- Living Legend Award, National Black Theatre Festival, 1993
- Claim Your Life Award
- WDAS-AM/FM, 1993
- Monarch Merit Award
- National Council for Culture and Art
- Pushcart Prize[7]

Nominations

- Tony
- Grammy
- Emmy award nominations (all 1977, all for *For Colored Girls Who Have Considered Suicide/When the Rainbow Is Enuf*)

Works

Plays

- *For Colored Girls Who Have Considered Suicide When the Rainbow Is Enuf* (1975) Nominated for a Tony Award, Grammy Award, and Emmy Award.
- *A Photograph: Lovers-in-Motion* (1977) Produced Off-Broadway at the Public Theatre.
- *Boogie Woogie Landscapes* (1979) First produced at Frank Silvera's Writers' Workshop in New York, then on Broadway at the Symphony Space Theatre.
- *Spell #7* (1979) Produced Off-Broadway at Joseph Papp's New York Shakespeare Festival Public Theatre.
- *Black and White Two Dimensional Planes* (1979).
- *Mother Courage and Her Children* (1980) Produced off-Broadway at the Public Theatre. Winner of a 1981 Obie Award.
- *Three for a Full Moon* (1982)
- *Bocas* (1982) First produced at the Mark Taper Forum in Los Angeles.
- *From Okra to Greens/A Different Kinda Love Story* (1983).
- *Three views of Mt. Fuji* (1987) First produced in San Francisco at the Lorraine Hansberry Theatre; first produced in New York at the New Dramatists.
- *Daddy Says* (1989).
- *Where the Mississippi Meets the Amazon* (1977)
- *A Photograph: A Study of Cruelty* (1977)
- *Mother of Courage and Her Children* (1980)
- *Whitewash* (1994)

Poetry

- *Melissa & Smith* (1976).
- *Natural Disasters and Other Festive Occasions* (1977)
- *Nappy Edges* (1978)
- *A Daughter's Geography* (1983)
- *From Okra to Greens* (1984)
- *Ridin' the Moon in Texas: Word Paintings* (St. Martin's Press, 1987)
- *The Love Space Demands (a continuing saga)* (St. Martin's Press, 1987)
- *A Photograph: Lovers in Motion: A Drama* (S. French, 1977)
- *Some Men* (1981)
- *Three Pieces* (St. Martin's Press, 1992)
- *I Live in Music* (1994)
- *The Sweet Breath of Life: A Poetic Narrative of the African-American Family* (Atria Books, 2004). Photography by Kamoinge [8] Inc
- *Enuf*
- *With no Immediate Cause*
- *you are sucha fool*
- *People of Watts (First published in Nov 1993 in VIBE Magazine)*
- *Blood Rhyhms*
- *Poet Hero*

Novels

- *For Colored Girls Who Have Considered Suicide/When the Rainbow is Enuf* (Shameless Hussy Press, 1976)
- *Sassafrass, Cypress & Indigo* (1982)
- *Betsey Brown* (St. Martin's Press, 1985)
- *The Black Book* (1986, with Robert Mapplethorpe).
- *Liliane* (1995)
- *Some Sing, Some Cry* (2010) (with Ifa Bayeza)

Children's books

- *Coretta Scott* (2009)
- *Ellington Was Not a Street* (2003)
- *Float Like a Butterfly: Muhammad Ali, the Man Who Could Float Like a Butterfly and Sting Like a Bee* (2002)
- *Daddy Says* (2003)
- *Whitewash* (1997)

Essays

- *See No Evil: Prefaces, Essays & Accounts, 1976-1983* (1984)
- *If I Can Cook You Know God Can* (1998)

References

[1] Lester,N: "At the Heart of Shange's Feminism: An Interview", Black American Literature Forum, 24(4): 717-730
[2] Felicia R. Lee, "A Writer's Struggles, on and Off the Page," (http://www.nytimes.com/2010/09/18/books/18shange.html) *New York Times*, September 17, 2010. Retrieved September 30, 2010.
[3] http://www.filmreference.com/film/63/Ntozake-Shange.html
[4] http://www.scils.rutgers.edu/~cybers/shange2.html
[5] http://www.bvonbooks.com/2010/10/15/interview-author-ntozake-shange-for-colored-girls/
[6] Blackwell, H: An Interview with Ntozake Shange," Black American Literature Forum, 13(4): 134-138
[7] http://galenet.galegroup.com.proxy.libraries.rutgers.edu
[8] http://en.wikipedia.org/Kamoinge

- Thomson, Gale. (2007). "Ntozake Shange". In *Contemporary Authors Online*. Apr 2008.
- Weaver, A . A. (2005). "Ntozake Shange Biographical Information". In *Women of Color, Women of Words*. Apr 2008.

Further reading

- Als, Hilton (8 November 2010). "Life and Letters: Color Vision". *The New Yorker* **86** (35): 42-47.

External links

- African American Literature Book Club: Ntozake Shange page (http://aalbc.com/authors/ntozake.htm)
- Rutgers University-Sponsored Ntozake Shange, "Women of Color/Women of Word" page (http://www.scils.rutgers.edu/~cybers/shange.html)
- Henry Holt Publishers: Ntozake Shange Bio (http://archives.obs-us.com/obs/german/books/holt/books/aloud/ntozake.htm)
- Multimanifestations: Ntozake Shange Page (http://www.multifest.com/poetry/shange.htm)
- "Color Vision", [[The New Yorker (http://www.newyorker.com/reporting/2010/11/08/101108fa_fact_als)] profile of Ntozake Shange by Hilton Als]

Tony Award for Best Play

The **Tony Award for Best Play** (formally, the **Antoinette Perry Award for Excellence in Theatre**) is an annual award celebrating achievements in live American theatre, including musical theatre, honoring productions on Broadway in New York. It currently takes place in mid-June each year.

There was no award in the Tony's first year. *All My Sons* has been incorrectly categorized as the Best Play of 1947, but it won the Best Author award for Arthur Miller. The following year *Mister Roberts* received the first Tony Award as Best Play. Authors and the producers are presented with the award.

Awards and nominations

1940s

- 1948: *Mister Roberts* by Thomas Heggen and Joshua Logan
- 1949: *Death of a Salesman* by Arthur Miller

1950s

- 1950: *The Cocktail Party* by T.S. Eliot
- 1951: *The Rose Tattoo* by Tennessee Williams
- 1952: *The Fourposter* by Jan De Hartog
- 1953: *The Crucible* by Arthur Miller
- 1954: *The Teahouse of the August Moon* by John Patrick
- 1955: *The Desperate Hours* by Joseph Hayes
- **1956: *The Diary of Anne Frank* by Frances Goodrich and Albert Hackett**
  - *Bus Stop*
  - *Cat on a Hot Tin Roof*
  - *Tiger at the Gates*
  - *The Chalk Garden*
- **1957: *Long Day's Journey Into Night* by Eugene O'Neill**
  - *Separate Tables*
  - *The Potting Shed*
  - *The Waltz of the Toreadors*
- **1958: *Sunrise at Campobello* by Dore Schary**
  - *The Rope Dancers*
  - *Two for the Seesaw*
  - *Time Remembered*
  - *The Dark at the Top of the Stairs*
  - *Look Back in Anger*
  - *Look Homeward, Angel*
  - *Romanoff and Juliet*
- **1959: *J.B.* by Archibald MacLeish**
  - *A Touch of the Poet*
  - *Epitaph for George Dillon*
  - *The Disenchanted*
  - *The Visit*

1960s

- **1960: *The Miracle Worker* by William Gibson**
  - *A Raisin in the Sun*
  - *The Best Man*
  - *The Tenth Man*
  - *Toys in the Attic*
- **1961: *Becket* by Jean Anouilh**
  - *All the Way Home*
  - *The Devil's Advocate*
  - *The Hostage*
- **1962: *A Man for All Seasons* by Robert Bolt**
  - *Gideon*
  - *The Caretaker*
  - *The Night of the Iguana*
- **1963: *Who's Afraid of Virginia Woolf?* by Edward Albee**
  - *A Thousand Clowns*
  - *Mother Courage and Her Children*
  - *Tchin-Tchin*
- **1964: *Luther* by John Osborne**
  - *The Ballad of the Sad Cafe*
  - *Barefoot in the Park*
  - *Dylan*
- **1965: *The Subject Was Roses* by Frank D. Gilroy**
  - *Luv*
  - *The Odd Couple*
  - *Tiny Alice*
- **1966: *The Persecution and Assassination of Marat as Performed by the Inmates of the Asylum of Charenton Under the Direction of the Marquis de Sade* (or Marat/Sade for short) by Peter Weiss**
  - *Inadmissible Evidence*
  - *Philadelphia, Here I Come!*
  - *The Right Honourable Gentleman*
- **1967: *The Homecoming* by Harold Pinter**
  - *A Delicate Balance*
  - *Black Comedy*
  - *The Killing of Sister George*
- **1968: *Rosencrantz & Guildenstern Are Dead* by Tom Stoppard**
  - *A Day in the Death of Joe Egg*
  - *Plaza Suite*
  - *The Price*
- **1969: *The Great White Hope* by Howard Sackler**
  - *Hadrian VII*
  - *Lovers*
  - *The Man in the Glass Booth*

1970s

- **1970: *Borstal Boy* by Frank McMahon**
  - *Child's Play*
  - *Indians*
  - *The Last of the Red Hot Lovers*
- **1971: *Sleuth* by Anthony Shaffer**
  - *Home*
  - *The Philanthropist*
  - *Paul Sill's Story Theatre*
- **1972: *Sticks and Bones* by David Rabe**
  - *Old Times*
  - *The Prisoner of Second Avenue*
  - *Vivat! Vivat Regina!*
- **1973: *That Championship Season* by Jason Miller**
  - *Butley*
  - *The Changing Room*
  - *The Sunshine Boys*
- **1974: *The River Niger* by Joseph A. Walker**
  - *In the Boom Boom Room*
  - *The Au Pair Man*
  - *Ulysses in Nighttown*
- **1975: *Equus* by Peter Shaffer**
  - *Same Time, Next Year*
  - *Seascape*
  - *Short Eyes*
  - *Sizwe Banzi is Dead / The Island*
  - *The National Health*
- **1976: *Travesties* by Tom Stoppard**
  - *The First Breeze of Summer*
  - *Knock Knock*
  - *Lamppost Reunion*
- **1977: *The Shadow Box* by Michael Cristofer**
  - *For Colored Girls Who Have Considered Suicide When the Rainbow Is Enuf*
  - *Otherwise Engaged*
  - *Streamers*
- **1978: *Da* by Hugh Leonard**
  - *Chapter Two*
  - *Deathtrap*
  - *The Gin Game*
- **1979: *The Elephant Man* by Bernard Pomerance**
  - *Bedroom Farce*
  - *Whose Life Is It Anyway?*
  - *Wings*

1980s

- **1980: *Children of a Lesser God* by Mark Medoff**
  - *Bent*
  - *Home*
  - *Talley's Folly*
- **1981: *Amadeus* by Peter Shaffer**
  - *A Lesson from Aloes*
  - *A Life*
  - *Fifth of July*
- **1982: *The Life and Adventures of Nicholas Nickleby* by David Edgar**
  - *Crimes of the Heart*
  - *The Dresser*
  - *Master Harold...and the Boys*
- **1983: *Torch Song Trilogy* by Harvey Fierstein**
  - *Angels Fall*
  - *'night, Mother*
  - *Plenty*
- **1984: *The Real Thing* by Tom Stoppard**
  - *Glengarry Glen Ross*
  - *Noises Off*
  - *Play Memory*
- **1985: *Biloxi Blues* by Neil Simon**
  - *As Is*
  - *Hurlyburly*
  - *Ma Rainey's Black Bottom*
- **1986: *I'm Not Rappaport* by Herb Gardner**
  - *Benefactors*
  - *Blood Knot*
  - *The House of Blue Leaves*
- **1987: *Fences* by August Wilson**
  - *Broadway Bound*
  - *Coastal Disturbances*
  - *Les Liaisons Dangereuses*
- **1988: *M. Butterfly* by David Henry Hwang**
  - *A Walk in the Woods*
  - *Joe Turner's Come and Gone*
  - *Speed-the-Plow*
- **1989: *The Heidi Chronicles* by Wendy Wasserstein**
  - *Largely New York*
  - *Lend Me a Tenor*
  - *Shirley Valentine*

1990s

- **1990: *The Grapes of Wrath* by Frank Galati**
  - *Lettice and Lovage*
  - *Prelude to a Kiss*
  - *The Piano Lesson*
- **1991: *Lost in Yonkers* by Neil Simon**
  - *Our Country's Good*
  - *Shadowlands*
  - *Six Degrees of Separation*
- **1992: *Dancing at Lughnasa* by Brian Friel**
  - *Four Baboons Adoring the Sun*
  - *Two Shakespearean Actors*

  - *Two Trains Running*
- **1993: *Angels in America: Millennium Approaches* by Tony Kushner**
  - *The Sisters Rosensweig*
  - *Someone Who'll Watch Over Me*
  - *The Song of Jacob Zulu*
- **1994: *Angels in America: Perestroika* by Tony Kushner**
  - *Broken Glass*
  - *The Kentucky Cycle*
  - *Twilight: Los Angeles, 1992*
- **1995: *Love! Valour! Compassion!* by Terrence McNally**
  - *Arcadia*
  - *Having Our Say*
  - *Indiscretions*
- **1996: *Master Class* by Terrence McNally**
  - *Buried Child*
  - *Racing Demon*
  - *Seven Guitars*
- **1997: *The Last Night of Ballyhoo* by Alfred Uhry**
  - *Skylight*
  - *Stanley*
  - *The Young Man From Atlanta*
- **1998: *'Art'* by Yasmina Reza**
  - *Freak*
  - *Golden Child*
  - *The Beauty Queen of Leenane*
- **1999: *Side Man* by Warren Leight**
  - *Closer*
  - *The Lonesome West*
  - *Not about Nightingales*

2000s

- **2000: *Copenhagen* by Michael Frayn**
  - *Dirty Blonde*
  - *The Ride Down Mt. Morgan*
  - *True West*
- **2001: *Proof* by David Auburn**
  - *The Invention of Love*
  - *King Hedley II*
  - *The Tale of the Allergist's Wife*
- **2002: *The Goat, or Who Is Sylvia?* by Edward Albee**
  - *Fortune's Fool*
  - *Metamorphoses*
  - *Topdog/Underdog*
- **2003: *Take Me Out* by Richard Greenberg**
  - *Enchanted April*
  - *Say Goodnight, Gracie*
  - *Vincent in Brixton*
- **2004: *I Am My Own Wife* by Doug Wright**
  - *Anna in the Tropics*
  - *Frozen*
  - *The Retreat from Moscow*
- **2005: *Doubt* by John Patrick Shanley**
  - *Democracy*
  - *Gem of the Ocean*

  - *The Pillowman*
- **2006: *The History Boys* by Alan Bennett**
  - *The Lieutenant of Inishmore*
  - *Rabbit Hole*
  - *Shining City*
- **2007: *The Coast of Utopia* by Tom Stoppard**
  - *Frost/Nixon*
  - *The Little Dog Laughed*
  - *Radio Golf*
- **2008: *August: Osage County* by Tracy Letts**
  - *Rock 'n' Roll*
  - *The Seafarer*
  - *The 39 Steps*
- **2009: *God of Carnage* by Yasmina Reza**
  - *33 Variations*
  - *Dividing the Estate*
  - *reasons to be pretty*

2010s

- **2010: *Red* by John Logan**
  - *In the Next Room (or The Vibrator Play)*
  - *Next Fall*
  - *Time Stands Still*
- **2011: *War Horse* by Nick Stafford**
  - *Good People*
  - *Jerusalem*
  - *The Motherfucker with the Hat*

References

- "Tony Award: Play" (http://www.ibdb.com/advSearchAwards.php). *Internet Broadway Database*. 2008. Retrieved 2008-08-21.

External links

- The American Theatre Wing's Tony Awards official website (http://www.tonyawards.com/)

Obie Award

The **Obie Awards** or **Off-Broadway Theater Awards** are annual awards given by *The Village Voice* newspaper to theatre artists and groups in New York City. As the Tony Awards cover Broadway productions, the Obies cover Off-Broadway and off-off-Broadway productions.

Background

The Obie Awards were initiated by Edwin (Ed) Fancher, publisher of *The Village Voice,* who handled the financing and business side of the project. They were first given in 1956 under the direction of theater critic Jerry Tallmer. Initially, only off-Broadway productions were eligible; in 1964, off-off-Broadway productions were made eligible.

Award structure

With the exception of the Lifetime Achievement and Best New American Play awards, there are no fixed categories and the winning actors and actresses are in a single category titled "Performance". There are no announced nominations.[1][2] Awards in the past have included performance, direction, best production, design, special citations, and sustained achievement. Not every category is awarded every year. *The Village Voice* also awards annual Obie grants to selected companies; in 2011, these grants were $2,000 each to Metropolitan Playhouse and Wakka Wakka.[3] There is also a Ross Wetzsteon Grant, named after its former theater editor, in the amount of $2,000 (in 2009; in 2011 the grant was $1,000), for a theatre that nurtures innovative new plays.[4]

Other awards for off-Broadway theatre are the Lucille Lortel Awards, the Drama Desk Awards, the Drama League Award, and the Outer Critics Circle Awards.

The ceremony for the 2010-11 season was held on May 16, 2011 at Webster Hall (New York City), hosted by S. Epatha Merkerson and David Hyde Pierce.[3]

List of winners

- Winners from Infoplease.com [5]
- OBIE winners, 2006-2007 [6], playbill.com
- OBIE winners, 2007-2008 [7], playbill.com
- OBIE winners, 2008-2009 [8], playbill.com
- OBIE winners, 2009-2010 [9], playbill.com
- OBIE winners, 2010-2011 [10], playbill.com

References

[1] Healy, Patrick. "'Ruined' Wins Obie Awards" (http://artsbeat.blogs.nytimes.com/2009/05/18/ruined-wins-obie-awards/) *The New York Times*, May 18, 2009
[2] Gans, Andrew. "Camp, Harris, Merkerson, Marvel and White to Present at Obies; Passing Strange to Perform" (http://www.playbill.com/news/article/116870.html), playbill.com, April 17, 2008
[3] Gans, Andrew. " 'Chad Deity', Ethan Hawke, Laurie Metcalf, Thomas Sadoski, Charlayne Woodard Win Obie Awards" (http://www.playbill.com/news/article/150893-Chad-Deity-Ethan-Hawke-Laurie-Metcalf-Thomas-Sadoski-Charlayne-Woodard-Win-Obie-Awards) playbill.com, May 16, 2011
[4] Cox, Gordon. Off Broadway event (http://www.variety.com/article/VR1118003900.html?categoryId=15&cs=1) *Variety*, May 18, 2009
[5] http://www.infoplease.com/ipa/A0153524.html
[6] http://www.playbill.com/news/article/108214.html$
[7] http://www.playbill.com/news/article/117880.html
[8] http://www.playbill.com/news/article/129344-Groff-Nottage-Sondheim-Cromer-Pisoni-Korins-Among-2009-OBIE-Award-Winners
[9] http://www.playbill.com/news/article/139593-Circle-Mirror-Transformation-Aliens-Metcalf-and-More-Win-OBIE-Awards
[10] http://www.playbill.com/news/article/150893-Chad-Deity-Ethan-Hawke-Laurie-Metcalf-Thomas-Sadoski-Charlayne-Woodard-Win-Obie-Awards

External links

- *Village Voice* Obies Archives of past winners (http://www.villagevoice.com/obies/)

Oz Scott

Osborne "Oz" E. Scott is an American screenwriter, television producer, film, television, and theatre director.

Biography

Career

Born in Hampton, Virginia, Scott attended NYU's Tisch School of the Arts and earned a MFA before he began his career in Washington D.C.'s Arena Stage. While at the Arena Stage, he managed the improvisational touring company The Living Stage. He then moved on to directing on and off Broadway plays including *For Colored Girls Who Have Considered Suicide When the Rainbow Is Enuf*, which earned him a Drama Desk Award in 1977. In 1981, he directed his first feature film, *Bustin' Loose*. During the 1980s and 1990s, Scott directed several television series and television movies including *Gimme a Break!, Scarecrow and Mrs. King, Crash Course, New Attitude, Civil Wars, American Gothic,* Lois & Clark: The New Adventures of Superman, *and* Providence.[1]

In 2002, Scott directed the VH1 television movie *Play'd – A Hip Hop Story* starring Rashaan Nall and Toni Braxton. The series went on to become VH1's highest rated program. The following year, Scott directed the Disney channel original movie *The Cheetah Girls*. Since directing *The Cheetah Girls*, Scott has gone on to direct episodes of *Strong Medicine, Everybody Hates Chris, Boston Legal, The Unit, Medium, CSI: NY,* and *NCIS*. In addition to directing, Scott also wrote episodes of *The Jeffersons* and served as supervising producer on two episodes of *The District*.[1]

In 2008, Scott was named the associate artistic director of the Negro Ensemble Company where he was also named to the board of directors.[2]

Personal life

Scott lives in Sherman Oaks, California with his wife with whom he has three grown children.[1]

Selected filmography

Director

- *Bustin' Loose* (1981)
- *Hill Street Blues* (1 episode, 1983)
- *Archie Bunker's Place* (1 episode, 1983)
- *Alice* (1 episode, 1984)
- *The Jeffersons* (2 episodes, 1984)
- *227* (3 episodes, 1985-1988)
- *Mr. Boogedy* (1986)
- *Fame* (3 episodes, 1986)
- *Bride of Boogedy* (1987)
- *Hotel* (2 episodes, 1987)
- *Dirty Dancing* (1 episode, 1988)
- *The Robert Guillaume Show* (1 episode, 1989)
- *The Cosby Show* (2 episodes, 1990-1991)
- *L.A. Law* (4 episodes, 1992-1994)
- *Picket Fences* (3 episodes, 1992-1995)
- *The Byrds of Paradise* (1 episode, 1994)
- *Northern Exposure* (2 episodes, 1994)
- *New York Undercover* (1 episode, 1994)
- *Party of Five* (1 episode, 1996)
- *Mr. & Mrs. Smith* (1 episode, 1996)
- *Lois & Clark: The New Adventures of Superman* (1 episode, 1996)
- *Diagnosis: Murder* (2 episodes, 1996-1997)
- *Chicago Hope* (2 episodes, 1996-1997)
- *The Practice* (6 episodes, 1997-1999)
- *Any Day Now* (2 episodes, 1998)
- *Spanish Judges* (1998)
- *Soul Food* (7 episodes, 2000-2001)
- *Family Law* (6 episodes, 2000-2002)

- *Ally McBeal* (2 episodes, 2001)
- *CSI: Crime Scene Investigation* (1 episode, 2001)
- *Lizzie McGuire* (1 episode, 2002)
- *Ed* (1 episode, 2002)
- *Dr. Vegas* (1 episode, 2004)
- *Kevin Hill* (1 episode, 2005)
- *The 4400* (1 episode, 2005)
- *Threshold* (1 episode, 2006)
- *Pepper Dennis* (1 episode, 2006)
- *Numb3rs* (1 episode, 2006)
- *Psych* (1 episode, 2007)
- *NCIS* (1 episode, 2008)
- *CSI: NY* (8 episodes, 2006-2009)

Producer

- *Bride of Boogedy* (1987)
- *The District* (2 episodes, 2003-2004)

Writer

- *The Jeffersons* (unknown episodes)

Award nominations

Year	Result	Award	Category	Works
1977	**Nominated**	Drama Desk Award	Outstanding Director of a Play	*For Colored Girls Who Have Considered Suicide When the Rainbow Is Enuf*
2004	**Nominated**	Directors Guild of America Award	Outstanding Directorial Achievement in Children's Programs	*The Cheetah Girls*

References

[1] "Oz Scott official biography" (http://www.ozscott.com/about/oz-scott). ozscott.com. . Retrieved 2008-09-03.
[2] "Major Producer and Director of TV, Film and Stage Joins NEC's 40th Anniversary Season" (http://www.reuters.com/article/pressRelease/idUS231100+04-Feb-2008+BW20080204). reuters.com. 2008-02-04. . Retrieved 2008-09-03.

External links

- Official site (http://www.ozscott.com/)
- Oz Scott (http://www.allrovi.com/name/p110575) at AllRovi

Article Sources and Contributors

For Colored Girls Who Have Considered Suicide When the Rainbow Is Enuf *Source*: http://en.wikipedia.org/w/index.php?oldid=429499903 *Contributors*: Alex contributing, All Hallow's Wraith, Bencey, Berkay0652, Bib, Bobibrown, Bookkeeperoftheoccult, Caltas, CameronTGD, Cgingold, Cirt, Countercouper, CrashCart9, Darrenhusted, Emerson7, Fluffernutter, Harddavid, ItsTheClimb17, J.delanoy, Jayy4life, Jezhotwells, Jmouse, John of Reading, Kikodawgzz, Lightmouse, LucentO, Mike Halterman, Miranda Stubbs, NerdyScienceDude, Nymf, OutriggerHawaii, PacificBoy, Scarmenkat, Ssilvers, SynthiaR, Tenebrae, The Anome, Treybien, Tshase, Vpw, 73 anonymous edits

For Colored Girls *Source*: http://en.wikipedia.org/w/index.php?oldid=456274260 *Contributors*: AbsoluteGleek92, Absurdist1968, Alansohn, All Hallow's Wraith, Arxiloxos, Bencey, Bender235, Big Bird, Bookkeeperoftheoccult, Bovineboy2008, Burlesquefastertang, Chris the speller, Cmart514, DD2K, Dovelyone, EarthSnow2, Ella Plantagenet, Froid, Gabe19, Giggles416, I dream of horses, InfamousPrince, ItsTheClimb17, Jagal85, Jarryl, Jayy4life, Kabulykos, Leszek Jańczuk, Lightlowemon, MikeAllen, Nymf, Paulp108, RBBrittain, Rich Farmbrough, Rjwilmsi, Ryulong, ScottMHoward, Suzannekarls, Tassedethe, Tom Danson, Tremorillo, Varlaam, Vchimpanzee, Volatile, Wiki972010, YNOTDNAANROL, Yougal500, 169 anonymous edits

Tyler Perry *Source*: http://en.wikipedia.org/w/index.php?oldid=463358866 *Contributors*: 12Msn34, 317twan, 5 albert square, 50%quick, A3RO, A520, A8UDI, ABCxyz, AMD, Academic Challenger, AdRock, Ada616, Adelson Velsky Landis, Adsmorrow, Afrokid245, Ahoerstemeier, Ajohnson4812, Ajpappal, Akeema200, Alansohn, Alchoska, Alex Middleton, Algebraist, Algetrig91, All Hallow's Wraith, Alloy, Alsocal, Amalthea, Amandastickettoride, American Eagle, Amourvocalist, Amyreelz, Angelo Michael, AniMate, AnonMoos, Antandrus, Anthon01, Arabbi, ArglebargleIV, Armyrifle9, Arthena, Arxiloxos, Asamadbhr, Asdflkjqwer, Ashmoo, Aspects, Aspireformore, Atlgirl052005, Augustlilleaas, Avicennasis, BW95, Baa, BanyanTree, BarryTheUnicorn, Beao, Bearly541, Belugaboy, BenSeattle, Bencey, Bender235, Bentogoa, Beyond My Ken, Bgranat, Bigar, Bigsean0300, BlackJAC, Blake Burba, Blogger9297, Bobo192, Bongwarrior, Borcat, Bovineboy2008, Brighat, BritneySpearsAddict, Broadway91, BrothaTimothy, Brown Villian 2008, Buda1701, Butros, Bzee91, CIreland, CR85747, Cabrosa, Caerwine, CambridgeBayWeather, Cameron Tate, Camilo Sanchez, CanadianLinuxUser, Canuckian89, CaribDigita, Carmichael, Cdpimpin2000, Ceanerob, Cgingold, Cheddarjack, Choalbaton, Chocolate tweety, Chowbok, Chris9086, Chrisjnelson, Chrislk02, Christian75, Christianster45, Chuck Baggett, Chuckiesdad, Ckatz, Closedmouth, Cmart514, Cmichael, Colin440, Colonies Chris, CommonsDelinker, Communitarian35, Condem, Corvus cornix, Courcelles, CowboySpartan, Cp4lyfe, Crystallina, D6, DFS, DJ Clayworth, DMCer, Daf, Damionbak, Damonsimmons14, Daniel, Danski14, Dante.antonio, Darklilac, Darwinek, Dasa098, David2032, Dbunkley6, Deloyd, Deconstructhis, DepressedPer, DerHexer, Diannaa, Dimakop, Discospinster, Dismas, Djcam, Dnvrfantj, Don4of4, Donmike10, Download, Drdstny, Dreadstar, Dreby14, Drmies, Duke100, Dutchmonkey9000, Dvyost, Dwayne, DynamoDegsy, DéRahier, E0steven, Ean5533, Ebp112002, Efreeman.fcg, Eivind F Øyangen, Ejfetters, Eleven even, Elliottsgay, Encyclopedist, EoGuy, Epbr123, Erebus555, Eric-Wester, Erielhonan, ErikNY, Erpert, Erudy, Esanchez7587, Esurnir, Etaon, Excirial, Explicit, Falcon8765, Fat&Happy, Favonian, Film2007, Firien, Flasunco, FlorencePS, Forbsey, Fraggle81, FrameWave20, Freepablo, Freiwilliger, FreshPineSent, Friginator, Froid, Frosted14, Funnyfarmofdoom, Galorey1, Gary King, Gemini531, Gene2010, Geniac, Gfdssfdg, Giordanobruno, GlaucusAtlanticus, Gogo Dodo, Goth67, Gowser, Grafen, GregorB, Gurchzilla, Gyro261, HJ Mitchell, HaeB, Hajatvrc, HalfShadow, Hanksummers, Happysailor, HarrisonB, Hiphats, Hirudo, Hispanicatthedisco, HitroMilanese, Hopkins75, Howieandkeyshia, I dream of horses, IW.HG, Idont Havaname, Imaginationac, Impactplayer, Inferno, Lord of Penguins, Ioio321, IronDuke, ItsTheClimb17, Iwrite2srt, Iyannaholmes, J.delanoy, J04n, JBsupreme, JForget, Jab843, JasonAQuest, Jauerback, Jaxsonista, Jbruin152, Jbstrevel94, Jennifargardinar, Jeztah, Jmabel, Joel Kirk, Joesphroth, John Reaves, John254, Jolomo, Joseramos3, Josh3580, Jpiece, Jredmond, Jujutacular, Kc12286, Keke101092, Kencaesi, Kendal Ozzel, Kevo23, Kidlittle, Kielz85, Kiconiadr, Kintetsubuffalo, Koavf, Kprice95, Krispy326, Kryptonian250, Kubigula, Kukini, Kungfuadam, Kuru, L Kensington, LaNaranja, Lady Mondegreen, Ladygreen, Landon1980, Landroo, Leonn97, LheaJLove, Lightmouse, Lilwoo93, Lima Neto, LindsayH, Lisapollison, Logan, LongDuckD, Loodog, LuisVilla, Luna Santin, Luwilt, Lvbrits, MSGJ, MSUDiva, MaJic, MafiaCapo, Makulman, Marek69, MarkMarek, Martarius, Marx01, Materialscientist, Maxviwe, Melbrooksfan101, Melsaran, Mentifisto, Mephistophelian, Metropolitan90, Michael Essmeyer, Michael Snow, Midamah, Mike Halterman, Mike Rosoft, MikeAllen, Mikeo, Minimac, Miranda, MissJanicka, Mistyblue2, Momoricks, Moriah93ohio, Motley Crue Rocks, Mouse Nightshirt, MovieMan123, MrKing84, Msshaden, Muffinator2.0, Muntuwandi, Murapai, Mykol, Mymyallen, N1RK4UDSK714, Naenae1996, Naniwako, Nathan, NawlinWiki, Nehrams2020, NellieBly, NeoSuperBlissey, NewEnglandYankee, Newsreader87, Nichole977, Nick, NickBurns, Night w, Nightscream, No One of Consequence, NorwegianBlue, Notedgrant, NotorSB, NuclearWarfare, Nymf, OGoncho, OMGsplosion, OOODDD, Officefreak, Ohconfucius, Ohnoitsjamie, Ojosbizcos, Ospalh, OuroborosCobra, OverlordQ, Ownflavor, P4k, PC78, Paime77, Paine Ellsworth, Parkwells, Paul Erik, Paulo Oliveira, Pb30, Pdcook, Penbat, Peregrine Fisher, Perez951, Peripitus, Persian Poet Gal, Peter Horn, Phantomsteve, PhilKnight, Philg88, Philip Cross, Philip Trueman, Picture Frame, Pigman5, Pinethicket, Pleasantview, Polo Montana, Ponyo, Profit22, QuasyBoy, RJASE1, Rainy1315, Raistolo, Rbrown9976, Rd232, Rdeluca03, Redvers, RexNL, Rhindle The Red, Robert Skyhawk, Robert Stephen Spiegel, Robofish, Robth, RockerGrrrl, Rogerd, Ron Ritzman, Ronhjones, RoyBoy, Rtab2, RussBlau, RustyShackleford12, Rwilliams214, Ryan the Game Master, Rzf3, S3000, SBaker43, Sailsbystars, Sam, Samast13, Satan Your Waiter, SatyrTN, Scanlan, SchuminWeb, Scimitar, Scooby7292, Scoochi2, Scottperry, Seahorseruler, Seaphoto, Senorbad, Sergay, Servedpancakes, Sfan00 IMG, Shadowjams, Sharkrocket, ShelfSkewed, Shell Kinney, Signshare, SkeletorUK, Skew-t, Skier Dude, Sldrgirl, Slowwriter, Smalljim, Smeggysmeg, Smilingsuzy, Snaxorb, Some jerk on the Internet, Son of Kong, Sourcechecker419, SpaceFlight89, SpacemanSpiff, Sposato, SpyMagician, Squandermania, Srikipedia, Ssor12, Staticshakedown, Staxringold, StephenBuxton, Stonnman, Storm Rider, Stwalkerster, SummerPhD, Swarm, Sweet xx, Swpb, T3chl0v3r, TMC1982, TPIRFanSteve, TallulahBelle, TamYum, Taywriter, Tbhotch, Tecb, Tempodivalse, Thatguyflint, The Iconoclast, The Moving Finger Writes, The Obento Musubi, The Thing That Should Not Be, The sobsister, TheLetterM, TheSuave, Thechillinvillan, Theimperial, Theroadislong, Thingg, ThinkBlue, Thomassz, Tide rolls, Tilla, Tinton5, Tktru, TnBsMommy, Tnxman307, Tombright, Tony1, TonyTheTiger, Tozoku, Tpbradbury, Tperrymovies, TracyLinkEdnaVelmaPenny, Trevor MacInnis, Trevy510, Trusilver, Turbogame, Twilightfan000, Twilite001, Twin11956, Txcrossbow, Ty3213, TyA, Tyciol, Tyler Parry, TylerPerry'sTylerPerry, Tylerdw, Udabest 01, Unedited, Undermedveten, Unionhawk, UnitedStatesian, Useight, Valfarly, Vanished 6551232, Varlaam, VenomousBeetle, Versus22, VictorianMutant, Vnjaus21, Volunteer Marek, WadeSimMiser, Waiting4acure, Walter Görlitz, Wapiko, Warut, WeevilKnevil, Werldwayd, WhartoX, Whitney.gracia, Wikidudeman, Wikignome0530, Wikipedian2, Wikipelli, WillMak050389, William Avery, Winchelsea, Wknight94, Woodstiger38, Woohookitty, Worldsfamous1994, Wowaconia, Wptoler, Xdenizen, Yamla, Yashar1, Youngandrestless, Zepeda, Zepheus, Zhou Yu, Zoe, ZooFari, Zoperd, 1854 anonymous edits

Trazana Beverley *Source*: http://en.wikipedia.org/w/index.php?oldid=399130590 *Contributors*: Emerson7, Kubigula, Tenebrae

Mariah Carey *Source*: http://en.wikipedia.org/w/index.php?oldid=463473488 *Contributors*: *drew, 13377331, 17Drew, 21655, 28421u2232nfenfcenc, 293.xx.xxx.xx, 2D, 2T, 3213212a, 5 octaves, 6afraidof7, 7swans, 97198, :etstaytogether, A Knavish Bonded, A Star Is Here, A p3rson, A vision of it, A3RO, AAAAA, AAFTSPOV, ABCD, ACSE, AJB4, AJCham, ARGOU, Aandrei, Aaron Schulz, Ababuj, Abog, Abu badali, Acalamari, Acetic Acid, Achitnis, Aczaxv, Adabow, Adam2981, AdamJacobMuller, Adambro, Adamisaiahgreen, Adamonline, Adashiel, Adi827, Adme2006, Aecis, Aef711, Ahoerstemeier, Ahruman, AimClover, Airbreather, Airjason95, Aitias, Ajwhales2007, Akamad, Akldawgs, Akuindo, Al-Andalus, Alai, Alarics, AlastorMoody, Albertoch90, Alejolo, Alensha, Alesachka, Alex250P, Alexandreblackburn, Alexandria, Alexf, AlexiusHoratius, Alfredosolis, All Hallow's Wraith, Allenk893, Allenwanghong, Alohawaiaoi, Alphachimp, AlyciaBellamyMediaInc, Amakuru, Amalthea, Amberrock, Ameki, AmiDaniel, Ampg1989, Ampotter, Ams80, Anarchristian, Anarchy 97, Anawrahta, And1987, Andre Engels, AndreaCarax, Andrew042886, Andrewlp1991, Andrij Kursetsky, Android Mouse, Andy 123445, Andy120290, Andypandy.UK, Anetode, AngelCrying, AngelOfSadness, Anger22, Angst72, Animesouth, AnnaP, Annalissette, Another Believer, Ansible, Antandrus, Antares33712, Antecreole92, Anthonyd3ca, Antifamilymang, Anywhere But Home, Aphordonte, ApnAEA, AppleIphone2010, Aquarising, Aragornthesquirrel, Arakunem, Arasthi, Arda Xi, AreJay, ArglebargleIV, Ariadne55, Artistopia, As00, Ashadeofgrey, Asher196, Ashleytisdale-cover, Ashton1983, Asifkhalil, Asnallar, Aspects, Aspern, Asphatasawhale, Ataricodfish, Atess, Atomic80, Attilios, AuburnPilot, Aude, Aurick, Autiger, Automatic, Ave120, AvestanHamster, AvicAWB, Avicennasis, Axiemeister, Az1568, AzaToth, Azcat1997, Aznboikent, B Touch, B0OP, BD2412, BJ Toxic, BMP87, BUF4Life, Babbs3777, BabuBhatt, Badagnani, BalticPat22, Balto9902, BaniHani, Baratayuda, Barista, Bart133, BaseballDetective, Baseballseries, Basilisk4u, Bassbonerocks, Batman Fan, Batxx, Bbatsell, Bdj, Bdushaw, Bealonzo, Beamathan, Bearcat, Beardo, Beetstra, Bejinhan, Belbo Casaubon, Bencey, Beno1000, Bento00, Besidesamiracle, Bgs022, Big Bird, Big Brother 1984, BigBrightStars, Bigglesthegreat, Bigjimr, Bigm552, Bigsean0300, Bilderbear, Billbort, Bille1028, Binary TSO, Binksternet, BirminghamUKDude, Biruitorul, Bisbis, Bitethedust, BitterMan, Bkabiri, BlackBurberry, Blackheartofgold, Blake Burba, Blanchardb, Blat!n0, Blobba, Blu Aardvark, Blueandgold200, Bluefizz32, Bluesatellite, Blueshatteredeyes, Bmascarenas, Bnguyen, Bobblewik, Bobo192, Bogdangiusca, Boi4mqnz, Boidiva02, Bon945, Bongwarrior, Bookkeeperoftheoccult, Bouncehoper, Boyblackuk, Brandmeister, Bratz angel14, Bree113, Brendansanatomy, Brexx, Brian the Editor, Brian0918, BrianMcM, Brighterorange, Brisvegas, Brody Brooks, BrokenSegue, BrothaTimothy, BrotherDarksoul, Bsroiaadn, BuickCenturyDriver, Bulldog73, Bulldoggie101, Bunchofgrapes, Buttered Bread, Butterfly52, C-squared, C777, COMPFUNK2, CRocka05, Ca luver, Caltas, Calvin999, Calvy.r, Camcallister, Camerong, Camptown, Can't sleep, clown will eat me, CanadianCaesar, Candii.licious, Caomhin, Capitalistroadster, Caprigol, Cardcapturs, Carefree Highway, Carinemily, Carlos1133, CarlosHernánChassares, Carpenoctem, Casey1817, CatherineMunro, Catsmartie, CattleGirl, Causa sui, Cburnett, Ccacsmss, Cearter1010, Ceauntay59, Cedrus-Libani, Ceedub88, Celebfanandy, Celeritas, Cenarium, Centrx, Ceoil, Cerasti, Cgros841, ChKa, ChaCha, Chairboy, Changstafolife, Chanlyn, Chantessy, Charlie Huggard, CharlotteWebb, Charmed36, Charmx12, Chasewc91, Chattwn legand, Cheifsguy, Chepetoño, Chevr92, ChiLlBeserker, ChicXulub, Chicheley, Chilvillow, Chiros Sunrider, Chmee2, Chochopk, Chowbok, Chris 73, Chris0619, Christopher Parham, ChristopherMix, Chronisgr, Chrysaor, Chsf, Chubbyblackblogger, Circles overyou, Circusstar, Cirt, Cjb028, Ck lostsword, Ckatz, Clausule, Clever boy who is smart, Cliff smith, ClockworkLunch, CloudNine, Cloveapple, Clovis Sangrail, Cmart514, Cmdrjameson, Cockinesss, Coffee, Colonel Warden, Colonies Chris, Colorfulharp233, Cometstyles, CommonsDelinker, Conversion script, Coojah, Cool Blue, Coolboy223, Coolhawks88, Coolkai, Cooly123, Corpx, Corvus coronoides, Coso 77, Courcelles, Courtberry, Couturecupcake, CovenantD, Cowman109, Cperea1994, Crazy in Love with Beyonce, Crazymansexyman, Crazyoldwoman, Cristina A. Bernardino, Crumbsucker, CryptoDerk, Crystal Clear x3, Crystallina, Ctprodigy7, Cubfan789, Cullen328, Curps, CutOffTies, CyanIsland, Cybercobra, Cypriot stud, Cytang, Czj, D6, DCEdwards1966, DLHH377, DRK, DRashadB, DStoykov, DVD R W, Da G007, Daabomb, Daal34, Daboy 29, Dac577, Daddy Kindsoul, Dado7, Dale101usa, DaltreyEntwistleMoonTownshend, Dalzzy, DamianFinol, Dan100, Dan33185, DancingPenguin, Dandvsp, Dangel326435, Dangerouslyinlove, Daniel5127, DanielBeaver, Danielv, Danotorious1jd, Danrivera, Danski14, Dante Alighieri, Danthetwat, Dantt777, Darena mipt, Darkone, Darksongbird, Darrenforster99, Dartg14, Darth Panda, Dasani, Dashit2, DaveMolyneux, Daven200520, David Gerard, David Rush, David Shankbone, Daviddaniel37, Dawn16, Dawnseeker2000, Db099221, Dbunkley6, Dcoetzee, Ddap09, DeJuanio, DeVante', Death of, Debbie33, Debouncer, Debresser, Deeceevoice, Dejsjs, Delldot, Deltabeignet, DennyColt, DerHexer, Destinyking, Devante12, Devona.westhaven asboro33, Dfmock, Dfrg.msc, Dgw, Diamond2, Diannaa, Diedoc, Digital Jedi Master, DigitalCatalyst, DigitalNinja, Dikeymikey, Dina, Dine club, Diphosphate8, Dirrtygirl, Discographer, Discovermine, Dismas, Disney09, Dmv74, Doc glasgow,

Doctorqui, Dollvalley, Dominichikaru, Donaldd23, Doodleboop, Dorftrottel, DoubleBlue, Download, Dpeters11, Dpstviva, Dragonslayer619, Drawme!park, Drawnunderwateryeah, Drdr1989, Dreaded Walrus, Dreadstar, Drindrin, DrippingInk, DriveMySol, Drivera28, Drmagic, DropDeadGorgias, Drpickem, Dskluz, Dspradau, Dswhite85, Dtowng, DwightHoward12, Dwonderful, Dysprosia, E. Ripley, E.B.I.V., EAB82, EHRLT, ESkog, EVula, Eagle Owl, Easterbradford, Ebp112002, Edwy, Eejhay, Efe, Efrafra, Ehtu, Eight88, Ejbaj, ElKevbo, EldKatt, Electric Storm89, Elemental5293, Elevation40, Elgrecoloco, ElinorD, Ella Plantagenet, Elmerson, Elyu, Emilee88, Emperor1993, Empoor, Encephalon, Endofskull, Endwar, EnterTheCircus, Enviroboy, Epbr123, Epp, Erarnat, Eric Bekins, Ericamick, Ericgo, Ericorbit, Erpert, Esanchez7587, Escape Orbit, Estheroliver, Eternal Equinox, Eurasian, Euryalus, Everyking, Explicit, Extraordinary Machine, Extreme Lopez Jr, F6Coloratura80, F9o0oly, FILWISE, Faethon Ghost, Fainites, Falcon9x5, Fallout boy, Fang Aili, FantajiFan, FantasyDreamloverForever, FastINCROYABLE, Fat&Happy, Fatso12345, Fattyjwoods, Faustlin, FayssalF, FeanorStar7, Feelgoodmusic, Fenwaypark89, FictionalCharacterGuy, Fifafifafifa, Filthyralph, FinalStrife7, Finngall, Fiona United, Firsfron, Fivedollarftlong, Fixedit1980, Fixer23, Fjeinca, Flamingspinach, Flojo2008, Flowerparty, Flyboy2200, Flyer22, Flyguy649, Fossils12, Fotooo4life, Fourthords, Foxcloud, Foxj, FraDany, Frankenpuppy, Fratrep, Freakofnurture, Freedomlinux, Freespirit1981, FreplySpang, FrickFrack, Fruarez, Funeral, Funguy06, Funky Monkey, FuriousFreddy, Fuzheado, Fys, GDonato, Gabe19, Gagayonce, Gaius Cornelius, Gamaliel, Ganfon, Gary King, Gary Kirk, Gaudio, Gaumaal, Gavatron, Gdavidp, Ge0fli, Gefflt01, Gemini86 618, Genghiskhanviet, Geni, Geniac, Genie, Genius235, Geoking66, Georgia guy, Gerards brother, Get2nomey, Getcrunk, GhenghisKharl, Giano, Gihad, Gil Gamesh, Gilliam, Gimboid13, Ginascrew, Girl Get it, Glane23, Glen, Globigloba, GnuDoyng, GoActive86, Gofastfast, Gogo Dodo, GoingBatty, Gokus Girl, Goodforlife, Goodgravy, Goolashfan, GotMilk3, GothGrrrl, Grace Note, Gracelouisad, GraemeL, Graham87, GrahameS, GreekStar12, GreenBayPackersfan09, Greg D. Barnes, GregAsche, Gregallz, Grey Pursuit, Greyserfer, Gscshoyru, Gsp, Gtg204y, Gtstricky, Guat6, Gubel, GuessWhoBatmann, Gurch, Guroadrunner, Gwernol, Gwnichols, Gzornenplatz, H, HJ Mitchell, HTurtle, Haemo, HalfShadow, Hall Monitor, HammerHeadHuman, Hansuum, Hao.ethz, Happyjam, Hapsiainen, HardCandy08, Harrisju, Harro5, Hashmi, Usman, Haxor1217, Hayden White, Haynsoul, Hecansing, Hede2000, Hekerui, Hell in a Bucket, Hello Control, Hello32020, Herunar, Heslopian, Heythere1234, HiLoser, Hiberniantears, Hill03, Hiphats, Hiphophomee101, Hirohisat, Hmains, Hog2, Hollow Wilerding, HollywoodIncfan, Honbicot, Honette, Honeydew77, Hoomanator, Hopeland, Horologium, Hotman2000s, Hotwiki, Hqb, Hqthief, Huangdi, Hulk, Hullaballoo Wolfowitz, Hungupbg, Husond, Hut 8.5, Hydnjo, Hysteria2424, I'll bring the food, I'mSimalicious!, I, Englishman, I-luv-bjork, IFixx, IJALB, ILoveDogz, INFO.MUSIC, INTERNE, IRP, IW.HG, Iamkkh, Ianjones1900, Ianjones50, Icey, Ifnord, Iggy Ax, Ignatzmice, Iheartedgar, Ihrtwiki, Ijjindos, Ikabod08, IllaZilla, Illinifan4192, Iluvbd, Imaninjapirate, Imbrown, Impaciente, Improve2009, InShaneee, IndigoYak, Infamous30, Ink Runner, Integla, Interestedscholar, Intime365, Inyrface, Iorsh, Iridescent, IronGargoyle, Ironflag1515, Irrypride, Is almeida, Itsbydesign, Ixfd64, Izno, J Milburn, J.MENSAH, J.delanoy, J04%h, JBZA2003, JDoorjam, JEMACAYU, JForget, JHMM13, JKevin01, JMK, JMSC88, JNFD, JPX7, JTSomers, JYolkowski, Jacek Kendysz, JackofOz, Jacoplane, Jacroe, Jagamijs, Jahiegel, JaimeAnnaMoore, Jalabi99, Jamaican g 89, Jamalar, James086, JamesAM, JamesBWatson, Jamesultrastar, Jampilot, Jan.Kamenicek, Jared martinez gwapo, Jasonglchu, Jasper Deng, Jasper420, Jasynnash2, Jauerback, Jaxl, Jay Pizz, Jay32183, JayFout, Jayandlaurabffl, Jayunderscorezero, Jayy008, Jayy009, Jcaragonv, Jcl32791, Jcrook1987, Jdude222, Jeff G., JeffHardy1Sabu2, JeffreyN, Jelly123455, Jemmabond, Jengod, Jennavecia, Jennica, Jerryseinfeld, Jes246, JesseGarrett, Jetblackheart, Jevansen, Jevives, Jeysaba, Jf nmgbjjml, Jgeszvain, Jheiv, Jhenderson777, Jibertiber, Jim Douglas, Jimarey, Jimmy Slade, Jittat, Jivesh boodhun, Jjasi, Jjmcspooh, Jjtm, Jkp44, Jni, Jnngjfgb, JoanneB, JoaoRicardo, Job, John, John Biancato, John Fader, John O'C, John Vandenberg, John of Reading, John254, JohnADean, Johnny0929, JohnnyRush10, Johnwporter, JonMoore, Jonathannew7, Jonhmayer-fã, Jonjames1986, Jonomacdrones, Joshafina, Joshstephen, Joshuajonajonathan12345, Joshuakeria, Joshyypo0o0, Jossi, Journalist, Jovanpopovic79, Joyous!, Jozsefs, Jpbowen, Jpo51, Jpoisson15, Jrog042003, Js2Jo, JuStar, Juandope, Judous, JuicycoutureGirly, Juliancolton, Julinho00, Junglecat, JustAGal, Jwad, K8 fan, KConWiki, Kali Max, Kandykane8816, Kanga1, Kansan, Karl1587, Karma Thief, Katalaveno, Katefan0, Katty77, KayBee45, Kbdank71, KelisFan2K5, Kelly Martin, Kellycya, Kellygirlaj, Kevoc, Khalif, Khoikhoi, KidOmega, Kieranj, Kikkokalabud, Kilby6, Kimiko20, King kong922, King of Hearts, Kingboyk, Kingcofield, Kintetsubuffalo, Kissfan1996, Kitchawan, Kiyoshi, Kleymannie, Klinean, Kmccoy, KnowledgeOfSelf, Koavf, Kodman, Kodster, Kompik, KooLKiiD, Koosh, Korg, Koshoes, Kowwin, Kozmic sk8r, Kpt2006, Kranberry506, Krellis, KriZe, Krich, Kriplozoik, Krissakristine, Kristelzorina, Kristof vt, Krychek, Kuk32483274, Kukini, Kungfuadam, Kurt Shaped Box, Kuru, Kww, Kyanez, Kyla, Kylemmenard, Kyorosuke, L Kensington, L&D, LAUGH90, LaTraviata1453, Laalaaa, LadyJ3000, Lakers, Lalonde, Lanairamaadlett, Lancini87, Lao Wai, Laps87, Lareine, Larry_Sanger, Larrybob, LauraAndrade88, Law Truth, Layladade, Lb34, Ld, LeLeHunt, Leafyplant, Leavin, Lectonar, Leebo, Leflyman, Legolas2186, Leroyinc, Lesanichelle, Lesliephung, Levelselect, Levineps, Lexlex, Licker245, Liffey, Lightdarkness, Lightmouse, Lights, Ligulem, Lil Flip246, Lil charm, Lil-muah, Lil-unique1, LilHelpa, Lilm901, Lilruthlessplaya, Linnell, Lino Mastrodomenico, Litefantastic, Little-al90, LizzieBabes419, Lliliany, Llort, Lmcelhiney, Lmherxon24, LnD DeLta FoRCe, Logsniffer1, Lone twin, Lookalikeaburger, Lord Moe, Loren.wilton, Louievuittondeeva, Louis Taylor, Loverboy012001, Lowellian, Lpgeffen, Lucas.tej, Luckyslimester, Lucy2006, Luigi-ish, Luke7059, Lully 2010, Luminum, Luna Santin, Lwuser2060, M A Mason, M.O.X, M2Ys4U, MADMADMAD, MCbutterfly, MECU, MER-C, MHeSong, MK, MKoltnow, MRGQ, MSGJ, MStraw, MaJic, Mackensen, Macutty, Maddyfan, Madoxxx, Maester Seymour, Magee2007, Maggott2000, Magioladitis, Magister Mathematicae, Mahalkitta, Mahdiislam, Mahogany h00r, Majorly, Malber, Malo, Mammamia9905, Mandarax, Mann.benoit@gmail.com, Manning Bartlett, Manumartinez 93, Mapsax, Marc-André Aßbrock, MarcK, Mareino, Mareklug, MariAna Mimi, MariaJaydHicky, MariahCarey, Mariahfanfan, Mariahicky, Mariahlyndell, Mariahpolen94, Marikology, Marioh13, Mark, Mark c08, MarkGallagher, Markj 87, Marleyluber, Marskell, Maryxpaul, Mason.Jones, Master Jay, Master Spider, Master&Expert, Master2841, MaterialGirl77, Mathvieira1, Mattbr, Mattbrundage, Matthew Yeager, Matthew hk, MatthewWaller, Matthewfox1303, Matticus78, Mattyboo, Mav, MaxPride, Maxim04, Maximus Rex, MayaSimFan, MayjahBLESyhu, Mayshaladi, Maythous, Mayumashu, Mcbridelr, Mcclel71, Mclambangel, Mcmarienez, Mcminno782, Mdchachi, Meeples, MegX, Megalodon99, Megan1967, Mel Etitis, Mentality, Merchbow, Mercurywoodrose, Meskida, Mezaco, Mhiji, MiMi-NyC, MicP, Michaelas10, Michaellennen, Michigan2101, Mickey gfss2007, Mickeymousechen, Midas touch, Mike Garcia, Mike Rosoft, Mike92591, MikeTuinstra, Milanov, Mild Bill Hiccup, Milkybar375, Millahnna, Milo Andreas Wagner, Mimi is cool, Mimibianca, Mimifan2006, Mindbender, Mindspillage, Minimac, Miranda, Mirzaz191, MisfitToys, MissParker, Misza13, Mizunoryu, Mkativerata, Mksmith, Mmgdertt, Mnemeson, Mocean, Moeron, MonarC25, Mono, MontrellDemet, Morwen, Mostaque99881, Moxy, Mr Minchin, Mr. Bouncy, Mr. Lefty, Mr. Sanchez 13, Mr.Z-man, MrFish, MrShamrock, Mrblondnyc, Mrzaius, Mshecket, Msjayhawk, Msmariahcarey, Msmonzi, Msp0, Mstatedawgs23, Mufka, Mumble45, Muntuwandi, Murderbike, Mushroom, Musiclover, Musicpvm, MuzikLuver, Mwanner, My76Strat, Mygerardromance, Myshaela, Mystic eye, Mystic27, N5iln, NOsRemLe, NRGKutKlose, Nack75, Najellin, Nakon, Nalren, Natalie Erin, Nataliemc, Nathan Hamblen, Nathan86, Natl1, Naurmacil, Nbagigafreak, Ncmvocalist, Neferuaten, Nehrams2020, NeilEvans, NeilN, Nekoangel17, Nem1yan, Nemo24, Netizen, NewEnglandYankee, Newgrumpyrad, Newsaholic, Newsmare, Nezumijin, Nfitz, Nica0827, Nick Linder, NickBurns, NickBush24, Nickjtorres, Nickvaldespino, NicolasJ., Nightscream, NikitaUtiu, Nine Tail Fox, Ninjawarriordex, Ninten, Nishkid64, Nnemo, No Guru, Nofoolz, Nofriendsx, Noozgroop, Norondor, Northside stl, Nothing444, Notwist, Novice7, Nowhy, Nrswanson, Nsaa, NuclearWarfare, Nunquam Dormio, Nwdavis, O-O Thatz b00bies, Oakpointballer, Offoaro1234, Ohconfucius, Ohnoitsjamie, Olijven, OmegaWikipedia, OmegaXmutantX, Omicronpersei8, Oncetum, One, One Sweet Edit, OneNamelessCat, Onioncows, Onislip, Only, Onorem, Oonthada, Op.mijn.werk, Opelio, Optimale, OriginalCyn3000, Ouseraquenao, Owen, P3net, PDH, PEJL, PTJoshua, Pabs1903, Pacholeknbnj, Paintballposer0, Palladium75, Palmlipbalm, Panda52, Paparazziboy1, Paragon12321, Passionvine, Pastafarian Nights, Patchiz, Patricio00, PatrickDion22, Paul August, Paul Barlow, PaulGarner, Pcpcpc, Pdcook, Pderrick13, Pearle, Pectore, Perceval, Perfectblue97, Perkyville, Peruvianllama, Petedogg1979, Petergriffin9901, Pgk, Phaedriel, Phatmonkey, PhilHip, Philbert2.71828, Philip Stevens, Philip Trueman, Philwelch, Phoebe tan, PhoenixPrince, Physcofreakretro, PiRSquared17, Piabelle, Piano non troppo, Piazzajordan2, Pic Editor96, Pilotguy, Pilun, Pineappletv, Pinkadelica, Pixelface, Pixelyoshi, Plek, Plkrtn, Plumphumps, Pmape09, Pmsyyz, Pobbie Rarr, PoloBox, Poopface39, Popiconmc, Possum, Postdlf, Prettybeautifulnailsalon, Prettyraya, Pridian, Pristinegoal, Private Butcher, Prof. MagneStormix, Prolixium, Psawyer1, Pteron, PucciniVivaldi, Puffinbuster, Pull Up To It, Pumpkinbootz, Punkymonkey987, Purgatory Fubar, Pushmybutton156, Pussypop, Pwnage8, QuadrivialMind, Quebec99, Quill, Qxz, R.aitken93, R00m c, RBBrittain, REGICUAZA, RJHall, RVJ, RachGreen, RadioKirk, RainbowOfLight, Rakesh32, Ramonthomas, RandalSchwartz, Randomtime, Rashawn1995, Raterr101, RattleandHum, Raul654, Raven4x4x, Ravenswing, Ravik, Raymondkeys, Rcababyjane, Rdsmith4, Realist2, Realm of Shadows, Reaper Eternal, Reaper X, Red-Blue-White, RedHillian, RedRollerskate, RedRose333, RedWolf, Redcomusic, Reddi, Redvers, ReganBoo13, Reidlos, RemoTheDog, Renaboss, Res2216firestar, Results May Vary 14, Retired username, Rettetast, Reuben Walton, RexNL, Rhindle, Riana, Rich Farmbrough, Rich4a1, Richard2201, RickK, Ricky81682, Rickyharder, Riddler921, Rightsaidfred, Rimmers, Rjwilmsi, Rmky87, Roadstaa, Rob411, RobbieNomi, Robert Foley, Robert K S, Robert McClenon, Robert Moore, RobertG, RobertMfromLI, RobertRay45821, Robinh, RobyWayne, RockMFR, Rodnee1977, Rodnee1978, Rodnee1979, Rodrigobeltransuito, Rodrigogomespaixao, Rogerd, RomanMC, Rommelo, Rory096, Rose64bud, Rosestiles, Rossrs, RoyBoy, Royboycrashfan, Rpbyrd3, Rrburke, Rror, Rs09985, Rshams2014, Rsolermo, Rsrwgwrgrwrg, Rtyq2, Rugops, Ruslik0, Russart 1999, Ruymi P3, RxS, RyanGerbil10, Ryanroy1230, Ryulong, S, SCEhardt, SColombo, SG, SKS2K6, SNIyer12, SOSOLAME, ST47, SVG, SWF Senior Trainer, SWT ANGEL, SallyForth123, Samil20, Sanbeg, Sancm7927, SandyGeorgia, SandyStrand, Sanfranman59, Sango123, Sanik79, Sarahlovsicecream, Sashak90, Sasquatch, Sassychick1898, Saucyminx, Savidan, Saz917, Scarian, Scary Boo, Sceptre, Scharles, Scherzinger Fan, Schmendrick, Schmiteye, Schneelocke, Schutz, Schwnj, Scumstache, Scwlong, Seb az86556, Sebizzar, Secfan, Secretss, SemiramideSutherland, Sensatez, Sephiroth storm, Ser Amantio di Nicolao, Seraphimblade, Sex 1234512345, Sexy Back 16, Shakesomeaction, Shakinharlem05, Shanel, Shanes, Shaneszukalski, SharkEmpress01, Shawn H. Meyer, Sheepshanx, ShelfSkewed, Shenme, Sherool, Shikinluv, Shimmera, Shirulashem, Shizane, Shomari16, Shoop85, Shshshsh, Shyam, SigmaEpsilon, Sigmundpetersen, SimonP, Sinceseems, Sir, Sir Nicholas de Mimsy-Porpington, SkateChamp80, SkyWalker, Skye 0913, Sl84, Slimepot636, Slon02, Smalljim, Smitty2k55, Sn0wflake, Snail2, Snail456, SnapSnap, Snoopable, So lonely17, So what, SoLando, SoWhy, Soapfan06, Sodaplayer, Softonic, Soliloquial, Solomon101, Solumeiras, Someareemoreequal, Someguy1221, Sonicseducer, Soosed, Sourcechecker419, Spammyou, Spangineer, Spark, Sparks Fly, Spellcast, Sphefx, Spilla, Splash, Spliffy, Sprinters1, SpuriousQ, SpyMagician, Srikeit, Sry85, Ss112, St3v3nb, StAnselm, Staffwaterboy, StarDeshay, Starcheerspeaksnewslostwars, Stardust6000, Starryland, Status, Stavdash, Staxringold, Steel87, SteinbDJ, Stephanp6, Stephen, SteveJ2006, Steven Zhang, StevenEdmondson, Stevertigo, Sthompson13, Street walker, Stretch 135, Strinbop, Stripes rule, StuIsCool, Stuartyeates, Sundar, Suomi Finland 2009, Suomi Finland 2009 test, SupaStarGirl, Suyw, Swainstonation, Swifferman, SwisterTwister, Syed Ahmad Al-Joofri, Syfuel, Syncere, Synthetic scott, Szyslak, T1980, TC89, TEB728, THE SLY, THISISME, TJRC, TMC1982, Ta bu shi da yu, Taksam, Taller is better, Tamati94, Tap jay, Tarret, Tarryn-jdj, Tarysky, Tassedethe, Tawon18, Taytay6666, Tbhotch, Tbo 157, Tctootall, Tdawgfive5six9, Tedy1girl, TeePee-20.7, Teenagebrand, Teklund, Teleyonce, TenOfAllTrades, TenPoundHammer, Tenebrae, Tennis Dynamite, Terence, Terra06, Terrence235, Teshik, Tevin27, TexMurphy, TexasAndroid, Tez1fl, Thalastmlw, Thankyoubaby, That Guy, From That Show!, ThatOneGuyFromWiki, Thatforumite, Thbuckland, The Almighty King, The Blizzard King, The Gnome, The Land, The Rambling Man, The Real One Returns, The Source of Wiki Power, The wub, TheBFunk, TheExecutiveWikiEditor, TheKid188810, TheKnowledge1814, TheQuandry, Thejdkkid, Thejjokerr, Theospence, Thepenguins, Theresa knott, ThisIsMyName, Thivierr, ThomasK, Threeafterthree, Tianxiaozhang, Tide rolls, Tiger71390, TigerShark, Tigermichal, Tim208, TimBentley, Timberframe, Timc, Timrock87, Tinton5, Tiptoety, Titoxd, Tjj348t, Tktktk, Tkurt, Tmac816, Tmt57, Todaealas, Tom.k, Tommy2010, Tonks, Tony Sidaway, Tony1, TonyTheTiger, Tonyauippa, Tonyvillagomez21, Toolboks, Toon81, TopopMAC1, TotalSpaceshipGuy3, Touchdown Turnaround, Toytoy, Tpbradbury, Tpetross, Trafton, Trampikey, Translucid2k4, TravisTX, Tregoweth, Trekmaster, TrentJones, Trevor MacInnis, Treyomarlorenztiptonforever12, Tribal44, Trichotomous, Trident13, Tristangaite-quiñones, Triste Tierra, TropicalMariahLover, Troynoble, Trusilver, Truthy not fakie, Tsp greenday, Tubeyoumania, Tuckero, Tukes, Turansuleyman, Turuncan, Tvgeek, Twistedslave, Twix1875, Tyrannitar, Tyrol5, UNITY99, UberVash, Ucanlookitup, Uglinessman, Ugur Basak, UkPaolo, Ulmke, Ulric1313, Ultimate Star Wars Freak, Ultimus, UltraRainbows, Ultraviolet scissor flame, Underneath-it-All,

Underorbit, UnicornTapestry, Unionofuranus, Unit22, Urinatorz, User2004, Ustyuzhanin, Ute in DC, V2007, Valanarra1, Valrith, Vary, Vega84, Vegaswikian, Veggiegirl, Velho, Velten, Veltron, Velvo, Venumb, Versageek, Vesta, Veteran dj, Victorshang, Videmus Omnia, Viennese Waltz, VincentG, Vints, Violinist1, Virangadippita, Vivalarey, Vizcarra, Vladsinger, Voceditenore, Voeidvectorcs1952, Vorash, Voyaging, W3stfa11, WIKIPEDIA FUCKING THE ALL, WLU, Wackiwikiwonka, Wacky 2004, Wafulz, Waldzazi, Wallie, Walmwutter, Wantobereporter, WarthogDemon, Wasted Time R, WatchAndObserve, Wayward, Wazza1, Wcwnwo17, Wcwnwo20, Wedineinheck, Welsh, Westfall, Weyes, Whatsmyname789, White Shadows, Who, Whouk, Wi-king, Wiccalrish, Wikaid, Wiki Raja, Wiki alf, Wiki edit Jonny, WikiArtifact, WikiCheckee, WikiLeon, WikiUni, Wikibofh, Wikieditor06, Wikieuphoria, Wikignome0530, Wikiking69, Wikipedia articles for analfuckbaggage, Wikipedia2006, Wikipediarules2221, Wikisanity, Wikiwikifast, Wildhartlivie, Will Beback Auto, Will2k, Willallen93, Willirennen, Willworkforicecream, Wimt, Winger84, Winhunter, Winick88, Winston365, Wisco, Wlgrin, Wmahan, Wo78, Woohookitty, Wrs1864, Wscott, Wtimrock, Wwfanz, X..sexispenci..x, XILE JOKER, XP, Xcali, Xeno, Xezbeth, Xiahou, Xinger, Xm2631, Xsharpshooter191x, XxJoshuaxX, Y ylime, YUL89YYZ, Yabaloo, Yamaguchi , Yamamoto Ichiro, Yamla, Ycarppi, Yinchongding, Yms, Yousou, Yrymar, Ytth, Yulia Romero, Yuoiuysdh, Yura`, Zabadinho, Zak 27, Zanapher, Zekosan, Zenohockey, Zetawoof, ZimZalaBim, Zimbabweed, Zippoist, Zoe, Zoeyk1, Zozza, Zscout370, Zumbo, Zzyzx11, , , 5490 anonymous edits

Ntozake Shange *Source*: http://en.wikipedia.org/w/index.php?oldid=462391766 *Contributors*: 87v7t76fc4iguwevf7657436253yd4fug754ws67dtfugiy67t8576, Alex contributing, All Hallow's Wraith, ArglebargleIV, Aristophanes68, BartlebytheScrivener, Bhoeble, Bill37212, Bobo192, CanadianLinuxUser, Cashthischeck, Cbustapeck, Ccson, Cgingold, Charles Matthews, Chemica, CycloneChibi, D6, Eastend, Elipongo, Godheval, GoingBatty, Henriettapussycat, Iago Dali, J. Van Meter, J04n, JaGa, Kc12286, Kikodawgzz, Larrykoen, Magicjewel, Mandarax, Mateosmuse, Mattconz, Misarxist, MuzikJunky, MylesCallum, Naijaliche, Ngulule, Papibear, Quadell, QzDaddy, Rboatright, ReadQT, Romais, Ser Amantio di Nicolao, Shakesomeaction, Smee, SouthernNights, Sunwin1960, TXFirebear, The Magnificent Clean-keeper, Tomkin, TreasuryTag, Woohookitty, Zero sharp, 68 anonymous edits

Tony Award for Best Play *Source*: http://en.wikipedia.org/w/index.php?oldid=442440257 *Contributors*: AdorableRuffian, Agnosticraccoon, Altenmann, Andre Engels, Antaeus Feldspar, Astorian, Barticus88, Bonuski, Bib, Canthusus, Capnpen, Chekaz, ChrisUK, Cleduc, Clossius, ColinFine, Colonies Chris, ConoscoTutto, Cowfrappe, Deb, Doh286, Emerson7, Fastfission, Flami72, Freakofnurture, FredR, Gadfium, Gaius Cornelius, Gap9551, Gareth E Kegg, Gongshow, Grenavitar, Grstain, Grsz11, Heck ja for ska, J. Van Meter, JanSuchy, Jeff G., Jerzy, Jiy, KF, Kikodawgzz, Laguna72, LiteraryMaven, Lugnuts, Martin TB, Mdukas, MegX, MovieMadness, Neddyseagoon, NightCrawler, Nunh-huh, Nyctc7, Orbicle, Oztotten008, PKT, Paralympic, Pegship, Psychadelicboy33, PunktKommaStrich, RedWolf, RickK, S.S. Miami, SFTVLGUY2, Saintrain, Sb1990, ShelfSkewed, Shortride, Stronach, Tassedethe, Ted Wilkes, Thepangelinanpost, Ulric1313, Urcolors, Woohookitty, 49 anonymous edits

Obie Award *Source*: http://en.wikipedia.org/w/index.php?oldid=457952204 *Contributors*: ARaleksandr, Ann.mclaughlin, Bearcat, Bib, Cirt, Emerson7, Flami72, Galliano7, Ganymead, GeorgeLouis, Hob, Homonihilis, Krossfire383, LilHelpa, Loginnigol, MFrog, MarnetteD, Michael Hardy, PerryDavis, Phaeton23, RedWolf, Saga City, SidP, Smee, The Thing That Should Not Be, TheLeopard, Thecurran, Tiger Marc, Varlaam, 13 anonymous edits

Oz Scott *Source*: http://en.wikipedia.org/w/index.php?oldid=462972537 *Contributors*: Artemisboy, Bender235, CutOffTies, Peregrine Fisher, Pinkadelica, QuasyBoy, WOSlinker, WikHead, 19 anonymous edits

Image Sources, Licenses and Contributors

File:82nd Academy Awards, Tyler Perry - army mil-66455-2010-03-09-180359 (cropped).jpg *Source*: http://en.wikipedia.org/w/index.php?title=File:82nd_Academy_Awards,_Tyler_Perry_-_army_mil-66455-2010-03-09-180359_(cropped).jpg *License*: Public Domain *Contributors*: 82nd_Academy_Awards,_Tyler_Perry_-_army_mil-66455-2010-03-09-180359.jpg: Sgt. Michael Connors - 302nd Mobile Public Affairs Detachment derivative work: Beao

File:Mariah Carey 2 by David Shankbone.jpg *Source*: http://en.wikipedia.org/w/index.php?title=File:Mariah_Carey_2_by_David_Shankbone.jpg *License*: Creative Commons Attribution-ShareAlike 3.0 Unported *Contributors*: David Shankbone

File:Mariah Carey 1990.jpg *Source*: http://en.wikipedia.org/w/index.php?title=File:Mariah_Carey_1990.jpg *License*: Creative Commons Attribution-Sharealike 2.0 *Contributors*: Redhoopoe at Flickr

File:Mariah Carey One Sweet Day Madison Square 1995.jpg *Source*: http://en.wikipedia.org/w/index.php?title=File:Mariah_Carey_One_Sweet_Day_Madison_Square_1995.jpg *License*: Creative Commons Attribution-Sharealike 2.0 *Contributors*: skinnylawyer

File:Mariah Carey12 Edwards Dec 1998.jpg *Source*: http://en.wikipedia.org/w/index.php?title=File:Mariah_Carey12_Edwards_Dec_1998.jpg *License*: Public Domain *Contributors*: Deadstar, Srbauer

File:Mcla re03.jpg *Source*: http://en.wikipedia.org/w/index.php?title=File:Mcla_re03.jpg *License*: Creative Commons Attribution-Sharealike 3.0 *Contributors*: taken by Steve Gawley

File:Mariah Carey 2003 tour 1.jpg *Source*: http://en.wikipedia.org/w/index.php?title=File:Mariah_Carey_2003_tour_1.jpg *License*: Creative Commons Attribution 2.0 *Contributors*: Scott Kinmartin

File:Mariah Carey in August 2006 2.jpg *Source*: http://en.wikipedia.org/w/index.php?title=File:Mariah_Carey_in_August_2006_2.jpg *License*: Creative Commons Attribution 2.0 *Contributors*: crossfirecw

Image:Mariah_Carey_Touch_My_Body_GMA_2008.jpg *Source*: http://en.wikipedia.org/w/index.php?title=File:Mariah_Carey_Touch_My_Body_GMA_2008.jpg *License*: Creative Commons Attribution-Sharealike 2.0 *Contributors*: all-systems-go at Flickr

Image:Mariah Carey Neighborhood Ball in downtown Washington 2009 2.JPG *Source*: http://en.wikipedia.org/w/index.php?title=File:Mariah_Carey_Neighborhood_Ball_in_downtown_Washington_2009_2.JPG *License*: Public Domain *Contributors*: TSgt Suzanne M. Day

File:Mariahparade1.jpg *Source*: http://en.wikipedia.org/w/index.php?title=File:Mariahparade1.jpg *License*: Public Domain *Contributors*: Petergriffin9901

File:Mariah Carey13 Edwards Dec 1998.jpg *Source*: http://en.wikipedia.org/w/index.php?title=File:Mariah_Carey13_Edwards_Dec_1998.jpg *License*: Public Domain *Contributors*: Anetode, Deadstar, Moonian, Srbauer, 6 anonymous edits

File:82nd Academy Awards, Mariah Carey - army mil-66460-2010-03-09-180308.jpg *Source*: http://en.wikipedia.org/w/index.php?title=File:82nd_Academy_Awards,_Mariah_Carey_-_army_mil-66460-2010-03-09-180308.jpg *License*: Public Domain *Contributors*: Sgt. Michael Connors - 302nd Mobile Public Affairs Detachment

License

Creative Commons Attribution-ShareAlike 3.0 Unported - Deed

This is a human-readable summary of the Creative Commons Attribution ShareAlike 3.0 Unported License (http://en.wikipedia.org/wiki/Wikipedia:Text_of_Creative_Commons_Attribution-ShareAlike_3.0_Unported_License)
You are free:

- **to Share**—to copy, distribute and transmit the work, and
- **to Remix**—to adapt the work

Under the following conditions:

- **Attribution**—You must attribute the work in the manner specified by the author or licensor (but not in any way that suggests that they endorse you or your use of the work.)
- **Share Alike**—If you alter, transform, or build upon this work, you may distribute the resulting work only under the same, similar or a compatible license.

With the understanding that:

- **Waiver**—Any of the above conditions can be waived if you get permission from the copyright holder.
- **Other Rights**—In no way are any of the following rights affected by the license:
  - your fair dealing or fair use rights;
  - the author's moral rights; and
  - rights other persons may have either in the work itself or in how the work is used, such as publicity or privacy rights.
- **Notice**—For any reuse or distribution, you must make clear to others the license terms of this work. The best way to do that is with a link to http://creativecommons.org/licenses/by-sa/3.0/

GNU Free Documentation License

As of July 15, 2009 Wikipedia has moved to a dual-licensing system that supersedes the previous GFDL only licensing. In short, this means that text licensed under the GFDL can no longer be imported to Wikipedia. Additionally, text contributed after that date can not be exported under the GFDL license. See Wikipedia:Licensing update for further information.

Version 1.3, 3 November 2008 Copyright (C) 2000, 2001, 2002, 2007, 2008 Free Software Foundation, Inc. <http://fsf.org/>
Everyone is permitted to copy and distribute verbatim copies of this license document, but changing it is not allowed.

0. PREAMBLE

The purpose of this License is to make a manual, textbook, or other functional and useful document "free" in the sense of freedom: to assure everyone the effective freedom to copy and redistribute it, with or without modifying it, either commercially or noncommercially. Secondarily, this License preserves for the author and publisher a way to get credit for their work, while not being considered responsible for modifications made by others.
This License is a kind of "copyleft", which means that derivative works of the document must themselves be free in the same sense. It complements the GNU General Public License, which is a copyleft license designed for free software.
We have designed this License in order to use it for manuals for free software, because free software needs free documentation: a free program should come with manuals providing the same freedoms that the software does. But this License is not limited to software manuals; it can be used for any textual work, regardless of subject matter or whether it is published as a printed book. We recommend this License principally for works whose purpose is instruction or reference.

1. APPLICABILITY AND DEFINITIONS

This License applies to any manual or other work, in any medium, that contains a notice placed by the copyright holder saying it can be distributed under the terms of this License. Such a notice grants a world-wide, royalty-free license, unlimited in duration, to use that work under the conditions stated herein. The "Document", below, refers to any such manual or work. Any member of the public is a licensee, and is addressed as "you". You accept the license if you copy, modify or distribute the work in a way requiring permission under copyright law.
A "Modified Version" of the Document means any work containing the Document or a portion of it, either copied verbatim, or with modifications and/or translated into another language.
A "Secondary Section" is a named appendix or a front-matter section of the Document that deals exclusively with the relationship of the publishers or authors of the Document to the Document's overall subject (or to related matters) and contains nothing that could fall directly within that overall subject. (Thus, if the Document is in part a textbook of mathematics, a Secondary Section may not explain any mathematics.) The relationship could be a matter of historical connection with the subject or with related matters, or of legal, commercial, philosophical, ethical or political position regarding them.
The "Invariant Sections" are certain Secondary Sections whose titles are designated, as being those of Invariant Sections, in the notice that says that the Document is released under this License. If a section does not fit the above definition of Secondary then it is not allowed to be designated as Invariant. The Document may contain zero Invariant Sections. If the Document does not identify any Invariant Sections then there are none.
The "Cover Texts" are certain short passages of text that are listed, as Front-Cover Texts or Back-Cover Texts, in the notice that says that the Document is released under this License. A Front-Cover Text may be at most 5 words, and a Back-Cover Text may be at most 25 words.
A "Transparent" copy of the Document means a machine-readable copy, represented in a format whose specification is available to the general public, that is suitable for revising the document straightforwardly with generic text editors or (for images composed of pixels) generic paint programs or (for drawings) some widely available drawing editor, and that is suitable for input to text formatters or for automatic translation to a variety of formats suitable for input to text formatters. A copy made in an otherwise Transparent file format whose markup, or absence of markup, has been arranged to thwart or discourage subsequent modification by readers is not Transparent. An image format is not Transparent if used for any substantial amount of text. A copy that is not "Transparent" is called "Opaque".
Examples of suitable formats for Transparent copies include plain ASCII without markup, Texinfo input format, LaTeX input format, SGML or XML using a publicly available DTD, and standard-conforming simple HTML, PostScript or PDF designed for human modification. Examples of transparent image formats include PNG, XCF and JPG. Opaque formats include proprietary formats that can be read and edited only by proprietary word processors, SGML or XML for which the DTD and/or processing tools are not generally available, and the machine-generated HTML, PostScript or PDF produced by some word processors for output purposes only.
The "Title Page" means, for a printed book, the title page itself, plus such following pages as are needed to hold, legibly, the material this License requires to appear in the title page. For works in formats which do not have any title page as such, "Title Page" means the text near the most prominent appearance of the work's title, preceding the beginning of the body of the text.
The "publisher" means any person or entity that distributes copies of the Document to the public.
A section "Entitled XYZ" means a named subunit of the Document whose title either is precisely XYZ or contains XYZ in parentheses following text that translates XYZ in another language. (Here XYZ stands for a specific section name mentioned below, such as "Acknowledgements", "Dedications", "Endorsements", or "History".) To "Preserve the Title" of such a section when you modify the Document means that it remains a section "Entitled XYZ" according to this definition.
The Document may include Warranty Disclaimers next to the notice which states that this License applies to the Document. These Warranty Disclaimers are considered to be included by reference in this License, but only as regards disclaiming warranties: any other implication that these Warranty Disclaimers may have is void and has no effect on the meaning of this License.

2. VERBATIM COPYING

You may copy and distribute the Document in any medium, either commercially or noncommercially, provided that this License, the copyright notices, and the license notice saying this License applies to the Document are reproduced in all copies, and that you add no other conditions whatsoever to those of this License. You may not use technical measures to obstruct or control the reading or further copying of the copies you make or distribute. However, you may accept compensation in exchange for copies. If you distribute a large enough number of copies you must also follow the conditions in section 3.
You may also lend copies, under the same conditions stated above, and you may publicly display copies.

3. COPYING IN QUANTITY

If you publish printed copies (or copies in media that commonly have printed covers) of the Document, numbering more than 100, and the Document's license notice requires Cover Texts, you must enclose the copies in covers that carry, clearly and legibly, all these Cover Texts: Front-Cover Texts on the front cover, and Back-Cover Texts on the back cover. Both covers must also clearly and legibly identify you as the publisher of these copies. The front cover must present the full title with all words of the title equally prominent and visible. You may add other material on the covers in addition. Copying with changes limited to the covers, as long as they preserve the title of the Document and satisfy these conditions, can be treated as verbatim copying in other respects.
If the required texts for either cover are too voluminous to fit legibly, you should put the first ones listed (as many as fit reasonably) on the actual cover, and continue the rest onto adjacent pages.
If you publish or distribute Opaque copies of the Document numbering more than 100, you must either include a machine-readable Transparent copy along with each Opaque copy, or state in or with each Opaque copy a computer-network location from which the general network-using public has access to download using public-standard network protocols a complete Transparent copy of the Document, free of added material. If you use the latter option, you must take reasonably prudent steps, when you begin distribution of Opaque copies in quantity, to ensure that this Transparent copy will remain thus accessible at the stated location until at least one year after the last time you distribute an Opaque copy (directly or through your agents or retailers) of that edition to the public.
It is requested, but not required, that you contact the authors of the Document well before redistributing any large number of copies, to give them a chance to provide you with an updated version of the Document.

4. MODIFICATIONS

You may copy and distribute a Modified Version of the Document under the conditions of sections 2 and 3 above, provided that you release the Modified Version under precisely this License, with the Modified Version filling the role of the Document, thus licensing distribution and modification of the Modified Version to whoever possesses a copy of it. In addition, you must do these things in the Modified Version:

A. Use in the Title Page (and on the covers, if any) a title distinct from that of the Document, and from those of previous versions (which should, if there were any, be listed in the History section of the Document). You may use the same title as a previous version if the original publisher of that version gives permission.
B. List on the Title Page, as authors, one or more persons or entities responsible for authorship of the modifications in the Modified Version, together with at least five of the principal authors of the Document (all of its principal authors, if it has fewer than five), unless they release you from this requirement.
C. State on the Title page the name of the publisher of the Modified Version, as the publisher.
D. Preserve all the copyright notices of the Document.
E. Add an appropriate copyright notice for your modifications adjacent to the other copyright notices.
F. Include, immediately after the copyright notices, a license notice giving the public permission to use the Modified Version under the terms of this License, in the form shown in the Addendum below.
G. Preserve in that license notice the full lists of Invariant Sections and required Cover Texts given in the Document's license notice.
H. Include an unaltered copy of this License.
I. Preserve the section Entitled "History", Preserve its Title, and add to it an item stating at least the title, year, new authors, and publisher of the Modified Version as given on the Title Page. If there is no section Entitled "History" in the Document, create one stating the title, year, authors, and publisher of the Document as given on its Title Page, then add an item describing the Modified Version as stated in the previous sentence.
J. Preserve the network location, if any, given in the Document for public access to a Transparent copy of the Document, and likewise the network locations given in the Document for previous versions it was based on. These may be placed in the "History" section. You may omit a network location for a work that was published at least four years before the Document itself, or if the original publisher of the version it refers to gives permission.
K. For any section Entitled "Acknowledgements" or "Dedications", Preserve the Title of the section, and preserve in the section all the substance and tone of each of the contributor acknowledgements and/or dedications given therein.
L. Preserve all the Invariant Sections of the Document, unaltered in their text and in their titles. Section numbers or the equivalent are not considered part of the section titles.
M. Delete any section Entitled "Endorsements". Such a section may not be included in the Modified version.
N. Do not retitle any existing section to be Entitled "Endorsements" or to conflict in title with any Invariant Section.
O. Preserve any Warranty Disclaimers.

If the Modified Version includes new front-matter sections or appendices that qualify as Secondary Sections and contain no material copied from the Document, you may at your option designate some or all of these sections as invariant. To do this, add their titles to the list of Invariant Sections in the Modified Version's license notice. These titles must be distinct from any other section titles.
You may add a section Entitled "Endorsements", provided it contains nothing but endorsements of your Modified Version by various parties—for example, statements of peer review or that the text has been approved by an organization as the authoritative definition of a standard.
You may add a passage of up to five words as a Front-Cover Text, and a passage of up to 25 words as a Back-Cover Text, to the end of the list of Cover Texts in the Modified Version. Only one passage of Front-Cover Text and one of Back-Cover Text may be added by (or through arrangements made by) any one entity. If the Document already includes a cover text for the same cover, previously added by you or by arrangement made by the same entity you are acting on behalf of, you may not add another; but you may replace the old one, on explicit permission from the previous publisher that added the old one.
The author(s) and publisher(s) of the Document do not by this License give permission to use their names for publicity for or to assert or imply endorsement of any Modified Version.

5. COMBINING DOCUMENTS

You may combine the Document with other documents released under this License, under the terms defined in section 4 above for modified versions, provided that you include in the combination all of the Invariant Sections of all of the original documents, unmodified, and list them all as Invariant Sections of your combined work in its license notice, and that you preserve all their Warranty Disclaimers.
The combined work need only contain one copy of this License, and multiple identical Invariant Sections may be replaced with a single copy. If there are multiple Invariant Sections with the same name but different contents, make the title of each such section unique by adding at the end of it, in parentheses, the name of the original author or publisher of that section if known, or else a unique number. Make the same adjustment to the section titles in the list of Invariant Sections in the license notice of the combined work.
In the combination, you must combine any sections Entitled "History" in the various original documents, forming one section Entitled "History"; likewise combine any sections Entitled "Acknowledgements", and any sections Entitled "Dedications". You must delete all sections Entitled "Endorsements".

6. COLLECTIONS OF DOCUMENTS

You may make a collection consisting of the Document and other documents released under this License, and replace the individual copies of this License in the various documents with a single copy that is included in the collection, provided that you follow the rules of this License for verbatim copying of each of the documents in all other respects.
You may extract a single document from such a collection, and distribute it individually under this License, provided you insert a copy of this License into the extracted document, and follow this License in all other respects regarding verbatim copying of that document.

7. AGGREGATION WITH INDEPENDENT WORKS

A compilation of the Document or its derivatives with other separate and independent documents or works, in or on a volume of a storage or distribution medium, is called an "aggregate" if the copyright resulting from the compilation is not used to limit the legal rights of the compilation's users beyond what the individual works permit. When the Document is included in an aggregate, this License does not apply to the other works in the aggregate which are not themselves derivative works of the Document.

If the Cover Text requirement of section 3 is applicable to these copies of the Document, then if the Document is less than one half of the entire aggregate, the Document's Cover Texts may be placed on covers that bracket the Document within the aggregate, or the electronic equivalent of covers if the Document is in electronic form. Otherwise they must appear on printed covers that bracket the whole aggregate.

8. TRANSLATION

Translation is considered a kind of modification, so you may distribute translations of the Document under the terms of section 4. Replacing Invariant Sections with translations requires special permission from their copyright holders, but you may include translations of some or all Invariant Sections in addition to the original versions of these Invariant Sections. You may include a translation of this License, and all the license notices in the Document, and any Warranty Disclaimers, provided that you also include the original English version of this License and the original versions of those notices and disclaimers. In case of a disagreement between the translation and the original version of this License or a notice or disclaimer, the original version will prevail.

If a section in the Document is Entitled "Acknowledgements", "Dedications", or "History", the requirement (section 4) to Preserve its Title (section 1) will typically require changing the actual title.

9. TERMINATION

You may not copy, modify, sublicense, or distribute the Document except as expressly provided under this License. Any attempt otherwise to copy, modify, sublicense, or distribute it is void, and will automatically terminate your rights under this License.

However, if you cease all violation of this License, then your license from a particular copyright holder is reinstated (a) provisionally, unless and until the copyright holder explicitly and finally terminates your license, and (b) permanently, if the copyright holder fails to notify you of the violation by some reasonable means prior to 60 days after the cessation.

Moreover, your license from a particular copyright holder is reinstated permanently if the copyright holder notifies you of the violation by some reasonable means, this is the first time you have received notice of violation of this License (for any work) from that copyright holder, and you cure the violation prior to 30 days after your receipt of the notice.

Termination of your rights under this section does not terminate the licenses of parties who have received copies or rights from you under this License. If your rights have been terminated and not permanently reinstated, receipt of a copy of some or all of the same material does not give you any rights to use it.

10. FUTURE REVISIONS OF THIS LICENSE

The Free Software Foundation may publish new, revised versions of the GNU Free Documentation License from time to time. Such new versions will be similar in spirit to the present version, but may differ in detail to address new problems or concerns. See http://www.gnu.org/copyleft/.

Each version of the License is given a distinguishing version number. If the Document specifies that a particular numbered version of this License "or any later version" applies to it, you have the option of following the terms and conditions either of that specified version or of any later version that has been published (not as a draft) by the Free Software Foundation. If the Document does not specify a version number of this License, you may choose any version ever published (not as a draft) by the Free Software Foundation. If the Document specifies that a proxy can decide which future versions of this License can be used, that proxy's public statement of acceptance of a version permanently authorizes you to choose that version for the Document.

11. RELICENSING

"Massive Multiauthor Collaboration Site" (or "MMC Site") means any World Wide Web server that publishes copyrightable works and also provides prominent facilities for anybody to edit those works. A public wiki that anybody can edit is an example of such a server. A "Massive Multiauthor Collaboration" (or "MMC") contained in the site means any set of copyrightable works thus published on the MMC site.

"CC-BY-SA" means the Creative Commons Attribution-Share Alike 3.0 license published by Creative Commons Corporation, a not-for-profit corporation with a principal place of business in San Francisco, California, as well as future copyleft versions of that license published by that same organization.

"Incorporate" means to publish or republish a Document, in whole or in part, as part of another Document.

An MMC is "eligible for relicensing" if it is licensed under this License, and if all works that were first published under this License somewhere other than this MMC, and subsequently incorporated in whole or in part into the MMC, (1) had no cover texts or invariant sections, and (2) were thus incorporated prior to November 1, 2008.

The operator of an MMC Site may republish an MMC contained in the site under CC-BY-SA on the same site at any time before August 1, 2009, provided the MMC is eligible for relicensing.

How to use this License for your documents

To use this License in a document you have written, include a copy of the License in the document and put the following copyright and license notices just after the title page:

> Copyright (c) YEAR YOUR NAME.
>
> Permission is granted to copy, distribute and/or modify this document
>
> under the terms of the GNU Free Documentation License, Version 1.3
>
> or any later version published by the Free Software Foundation;
>
> with no Invariant Sections, no Front-Cover Texts, and no Back-Cover Texts.
>
> A copy of the license is included in the section entitled "GNU
>
> Free Documentation License".

If you have Invariant Sections, Front-Cover Texts and Back-Cover Texts, replace the "with...Texts." line with this:

> with the Invariant Sections being LIST THEIR TITLES, with the
>
> Front-Cover Texts being LIST, and with the Back-Cover Texts being LIST.

If you have Invariant Sections without Cover Texts, or some other combination of the three, merge those two alternatives to suit the situation.

If your document contains nontrivial examples of program code, we recommend releasing these examples in parallel under your choice of free software license, such as the GNU General Public License, to permit their use in free software.

Creative Commons Attribution-ShareAlike 3.0 Unported License

CREATIVE COMMONS CORPORATION IS NOT A LAW FIRM AND DOES NOT PROVIDE LEGAL SERVICES. DISTRIBUTION OF THIS LICENSE DOES NOT CREATE AN ATTORNEY-CLIENT RELATIONSHIP. CREATIVE COMMONS PROVIDES THIS INFORMATION ON AN «AS-IS» BASIS. CREATIVE COMMONS MAKES NO WARRANTIES REGARDING THE INFORMATION PROVIDED, AND DISCLAIMS LIABILITY FOR DAMAGES RESULTING FROM ITS USE.

License

THE WORK (AS DEFINED BELOW) IS PROVIDED UNDER THE TERMS OF THIS CREATIVE COMMONS PUBLIC LICENSE («CCPL» OR «LICENSE»). THE WORK IS PROTECTED BY COPYRIGHT AND/OR OTHER APPLICABLE LAW. ANY USE OF THE WORK OTHER THAN AS AUTHORIZED UNDER THIS LICENSE OR COPYRIGHT LAW IS PROHIBITED.

BY EXERCISING ANY RIGHTS TO THE WORK PROVIDED HERE, YOU ACCEPT AND AGREE TO BE BOUND BY THE TERMS OF THIS LICENSE. TO THE EXTENT THIS LICENSE MAY BE CONSIDERED TO BE A CONTRACT, THE LICENSOR GRANTS YOU THE RIGHTS CONTAINED HERE IN CONSIDERATION OF YOUR ACCEPTANCE OF SUCH TERMS AND CONDITIONS.

1. Definitions

"Adaptation" means a work based upon the Work, or upon the Work and other pre-existing works, such as a translation, adaptation, derivative work, arrangement of music or other alterations of a literary or artistic work, or phonogram or performance and includes cinematographic adaptations or any other form in which the Work may be recast, transformed, or adapted including in any form recognizably derived from the original, except that a work that constitutes a Collection will not be considered an Adaptation for the purpose of this License. For the avoidance of doubt, where the Work is a musical work, performance or phonogram, the synchronization of the Work in timed-relation with a moving image ("synching") will be considered an Adaptation for the purpose of this License.

"Collection" means a collection of literary or artistic works, such as encyclopedias and anthologies, or performances, phonograms or broadcasts, or other works or subject matter other than works listed in Section 1(f) below, which, by reason of the selection and arrangement of their contents, constitute intellectual creations, in which the Work is included in its entirety in unmodified form along with one or more other contributions, each constituting separate and independent works in themselves, which together are assembled into a collective whole. A work that constitutes a Collection will not be considered an Adaptation (as defined below) for the purposes of this License.

"Creative Commons Compatible License" means a license that is listed at http://creativecommons.org/compatiblelicenses that has been approved by Creative Commons as being essentially equivalent to this License, including, at a minimum, because that license: (i) contains terms that have the same purpose, meaning and effect as the License Elements of this License; and, (ii) explicitly permits the relicensing of adaptations of works made available under that license under this License or a Creative Commons jurisdiction license with the same License Elements as this License.

"Distribute" means to make available to the public the original and copies of the Work or Adaptation, as appropriate, through sale or other transfer of ownership.

"License Elements" means the following high-level license attributes as selected by Licensor and indicated in the title of this License: Attribution, ShareAlike.

"Licensor" means the individual, individuals, entity or entities that offer(s) the Work under the terms of this License.

"Original Author" means, in the case of a literary or artistic work, the individual, individuals, entity or entities who created the Work or if no individual or entity can be identified, the publisher; and in addition (i) in the case of a performance the actors, singers, musicians, dancers, and other persons who act, sing, deliver, declaim, play in, interpret or otherwise perform literary or artistic works or expressions of folklore; (ii) in the case of a phonogram the producer being the person or legal entity who first fixes the sounds of a performance or other sounds; and, (iii) in the case of broadcasts, the organization that transmits the broadcast.

"Work" means the literary and/or artistic work offered under the terms of this License including without limitation any production in the literary, scientific and artistic domain, whatever may be the mode or form of its expression including digital form, such as a book, pamphlet and other writing; a lecture, address, sermon or other work of the same nature; a dramatic or dramatico-musical work; a choreographic work or entertainment in dumb show; a musical composition with or without words; a cinematographic work to which are assimilated works expressed by a process analogous to cinematography; a work of drawing, painting, architecture, sculpture, engraving or lithography; a photographic work to which are assimilated works expressed by a process analogous to photography; a work of applied art; an illustration, map, plan, sketch or three-dimensional work relative to geography, topography, architecture or science; a performance; a broadcast; a phonogram; a compilation of data to the extent it is protected as a copyrightable work; or a work performed by a variety or circus performer to the extent it is not otherwise considered a literary or artistic work.

"You" means an individual or entity exercising rights under this License who has not previously violated the terms of this License with respect to the Work, or who has received express permission from the Licensor to exercise rights under this License despite a previous violation.

"Publicly Perform" means to perform public recitations of the Work and to communicate to the public those public recitations, by any means or process, including by wire or wireless means or public digital performances; to make available to the public Works in such a way that members of the public may access these Works from a place and at a place individually chosen by them; to perform the Work to the public by any means or process and the communication to the public of the performances of the Work, including by public digital performance; to broadcast and rebroadcast the Work by any means including signs, sounds or images.

"Reproduce" means to make copies of the Work by any means including without limitation by sound or visual recordings and the right of fixation and reproducing fixations of the Work, including storage of a protected performance or phonogram in digital form or other electronic medium.

2. Fair Dealing Rights

Nothing in this License is intended to reduce, limit, or restrict any uses free from copyright or rights arising from limitations or exceptions that are provided for in connection with the copyright protection under copyright law or other applicable laws.

3. License Grant

Subject to the terms and conditions of this License, Licensor hereby grants You a worldwide, royalty-free, non-exclusive, perpetual (for the duration of the applicable copyright) license to exercise the rights in the Work as stated below:

a. to Reproduce the Work, to incorporate the Work into one or more Collections, and to Reproduce the Work as incorporated in the Collections;

b. to create and Reproduce Adaptations provided that any such Adaptation, including any translation in any medium, takes reasonable steps to clearly label, demarcate or otherwise identify that changes were made to the original Work. For example, a translation could be marked "The original work was translated from English to Spanish," or a modification could indicate "The original work has been modified.";

c. to Distribute and Publicly Perform the Work including as incorporated in Collections; and,

d. to Distribute and Publicly Perform Adaptations.

e. For the avoidance of doubt:

vi. **Non-waivable Compulsory License Schemes.** In those jurisdictions in which the right to collect royalties through any statutory or compulsory licensing scheme cannot be waived, the Licensor reserves the exclusive right to collect such royalties for any exercise by You of the rights granted under this License;

vii. **Waivable Compulsory License Schemes.** In those jurisdictions in which the right to collect royalties through any statutory or compulsory licensing scheme can be waived, the Licensor waives the exclusive right to collect such royalties for any exercise by You of the rights granted under this License; and,

viii. **Voluntary License Schemes.** The Licensor waives the right to collect royalties, whether individually or, in the event that the Licensor is a member of a collecting society that administers voluntary licensing schemes, via that society, from any exercise by You of the rights granted under this License.

The above rights may be exercised in all media and formats whether now known or hereafter devised. The above rights include the right to make such modifications as are technically necessary to exercise the rights in other media and formats. Subject to Section 8(f), all rights not expressly granted by Licensor are hereby reserved.

4. Restrictions

The license granted in Section 3 above is expressly made subject to and limited by the following restrictions:

a. You may Distribute or Publicly Perform the Work only under the terms of this License. You must include a copy of, or the Uniform Resource Identifier (URI) for, this License with every copy of the Work You Distribute or Publicly Perform. You may not offer or impose any terms on the Work that restrict the terms of this License or the ability of the recipient of the Work to exercise the rights granted to that recipient under the terms of the License. You may not sublicense the Work. You must keep intact all notices that refer to this License and to the disclaimer of warranties with every copy of the Work You Distribute or Publicly Perform. When You Distribute or Publicly Perform the Work, You may not impose any effective technological measures on the Work that restrict the ability of a recipient of the Work from You to exercise the rights granted to that recipient under the terms of the License. This Section 4(a) applies to the Work as incorporated in a Collection, but this does not require the Collection apart from the Work itself to be made subject to the terms of this License. If You create a Collection, upon notice from any Licensor You must, to the extent practicable, remove from the Collection any credit as required by Section 4(c), as requested. If You create an Adaptation, upon notice from any Licensor You must, to the extent practicable, remove from the Adaptation any credit as required by Section 4(c), as requested.

b. You may Distribute or Publicly Perform an Adaptation only under the terms of: (i) this License; (ii) a later version of this License with the same License Elements as this License; (iii) a Creative Commons jurisdiction license (either this or a later license version) that contains the same License Elements as this License (e.g., Attribution-ShareAlike 3.0 US)); (iv) a Creative Commons Compatible License. If you license the Adaptation under one of the licenses mentioned in (iv), you must comply with the terms of that license. If you license the Adaptation under the terms of any of the licenses mentioned in (i), (ii) or (iii) (the "Applicable License"), you must comply with the terms of the Applicable License generally and the following provisions: (I) You must include a copy of, or the URI for, the Applicable License with every copy of each Adaptation You Distribute or Publicly Perform; (II) You may not offer or impose any terms on the Adaptation that restrict the terms of the Applicable License or the ability of the recipient of the Adaptation to exercise the rights granted to that recipient under the terms of the Applicable License; (III) You must keep intact all notices that refer to the Applicable License and to the disclaimer of warranties with every copy of the Work as included in the Adaptation You Distribute or Publicly Perform; (IV) when You Distribute or Publicly Perform the Adaptation, You may not impose any effective technological measures on the Adaptation that restrict the ability of a recipient of the Adaptation from You to exercise the rights granted to that recipient under the terms of the Applicable License. This Section 4(b) applies to the Adaptation as incorporated in a Collection, but this does not require the Collection apart from the Adaptation itself to be made subject to the terms of the Applicable License.

c. If You Distribute, or Publicly Perform the Work or any Adaptations or Collections, You must, unless a request has been made pursuant to Section 4(a), keep intact all copyright notices for the Work and provide, reasonable to the medium or means You are utilizing: (i) the name of the Original Author (or pseudonym, if applicable) if supplied, and/or if the Original Author and/or Licensor designate another party or parties (e.g., a sponsor institute, publishing entity, journal) for attribution ("Attribution Parties") in Licensor's copyright notice, terms of service or by other reasonable means, the name of such party or parties; (ii) the title of the Work if supplied; (iii) to the extent reasonably practicable, the URI, if any, that Licensor specifies to be associated with the Work, unless such URI does not refer to the copyright notice or licensing information for the Work; and (iv) , consistent with Section 3(b), in the case of an Adaptation, a credit identifying the use of the Work in the Adaptation (e.g., "French translation of the Work by Original Author," or "Screenplay based on original Work by Original Author"). The credit required by this Section 4(c) may be implemented in any reasonable manner; provided, however, that in the case of a Adaptation or Collection, at a minimum such credit will appear, if a credit for all contributing authors of the Adaptation or Collection appears, then as part of these credits and in a manner at least as prominent as the credits for the other contributing authors. For the avoidance of doubt, You may only use the credit required by this Section for the purpose of attribution in the manner set out above and, by exercising Your rights under this License, You may not implicitly or explicitly assert or imply any connection with, sponsorship or endorsement by the Original Author, Licensor and/or Attribution Parties, as appropriate, of You or Your use of the Work, without the separate, express prior written permission of the Original Author, Licensor and/or Attribution Parties.

d. Except as otherwise agreed in writing by the Licensor or as may be otherwise permitted by applicable law, if You Reproduce, Distribute or Publicly Perform the Work either by itself or as part of any Adaptations or Collections, You must not distort, mutilate, modify or take other derogatory action in relation to the Work which would be prejudicial to the Original Author's honor or reputation. Licensor agrees that in those jurisdictions (e.g. Japan), in which any exercise of the right granted in Section 3(b) of this License (the right to make Adaptations) would be deemed to be a distortion, mutilation, modification or other derogatory action prejudicial to the Original Author's honor and reputation, the Licensor will waive or not assert, as appropriate, this Section, to the fullest extent permitted by the applicable national law, to enable You to reasonably exercise Your right under Section 3(b) of this License (right to make Adaptations) but not otherwise.

5. Representations, Warranties and Disclaimer

UNLESS OTHERWISE MUTUALLY AGREED TO BY THE PARTIES IN WRITING, LICENSOR OFFERS THE WORK AS-IS AND MAKES NO REPRESENTATIONS OR WARRANTIES OF ANY KIND CONCERNING THE WORK, EXPRESS, IMPLIED, STATUTORY OR OTHERWISE, INCLUDING, WITHOUT LIMITATION, WARRANTIES OF TITLE, MERCHANTIBILITY, FITNESS FOR A PARTICULAR PURPOSE, NONINFRINGEMENT, OR THE ABSENCE OF LATENT OR OTHER DEFECTS, ACCURACY, OR THE PRESENCE OF ABSENCE OF ERRORS, WHETHER OR NOT DISCOVERABLE. SOME JURISDICTIONS DO NOT ALLOW THE EXCLUSION OF IMPLIED WARRANTIES, SO SUCH EXCLUSION MAY NOT APPLY TO YOU.

6. Limitation on Liability

EXCEPT TO THE EXTENT REQUIRED BY APPLICABLE LAW, IN NO EVENT WILL LICENSOR BE LIABLE TO YOU ON ANY LEGAL THEORY FOR ANY SPECIAL, INCIDENTAL, CONSEQUENTIAL, PUNITIVE OR EXEMPLARY DAMAGES ARISING OUT OF THIS LICENSE OR THE USE OF THE WORK, EVEN IF LICENSOR HAS BEEN ADVISED OF THE POSSIBILITY OF SUCH DAMAGES.

7. Termination

a. This License and the rights granted hereunder will terminate automatically upon any breach by You of the terms of this License. Individuals or entities who have received Adaptations or Collections from You under this License, however, will not have their licenses terminated provided such individuals or entities remain in full compliance with those licenses. Sections 1, 2, 5, 6, 7, and 8 will survive any termination of this License.

b. Subject to the above terms and conditions, the license granted here is perpetual (for the duration of the applicable copyright in the Work). Notwithstanding the above, Licensor reserves the right to release the Work under different license terms or to stop distributing the Work at any time; provided, however that any such election will not serve to withdraw this License (or any other license that has been, or is required to be, granted under the terms of this License), and this License will continue in full force and effect unless terminated as stated above.

8. Miscellaneous

a. Each time You Distribute or Publicly Perform the Work or a Collection, the Licensor offers to the recipient a license to the Work on the same terms and conditions as the license granted to You under this License.

b. Each time You Distribute or Publicly Perform an Adaptation, Licensor offers to the recipient a license to the original Work on the same terms and conditions as the license granted to You under this License.

c. If any provision of this License is invalid or unenforceable under applicable law, it shall not affect the validity or enforceability of the remainder of the terms of this License, and without further action by the parties to this agreement, such provision shall be reformed to the minimum extent necessary to make such provision valid and enforceable.

d. No term or provision of this License shall be deemed waived and no breach consented to unless such waiver or consent shall be in writing and signed by the party to be charged with such waiver or consent.

e. This License constitutes the entire agreement between the parties with respect to the Work licensed here. There are no understandings, agreements or representations with respect to the Work not specified here. Licensor shall not be bound by any additional provisions that may appear in any communication from You. This License may not be modified without the mutual written agreement of the Licensor and You.

f. The rights granted under, and the subject matter referenced, in this License were drafted utilizing the terminology of the Berne Convention for the Protection of Literary and Artistic Works (as amended on September 28, 1979), the Rome Convention of 1961, the WIPO Copyright Treaty of 1996, the WIPO Performances and Phonograms Treaty of 1996 and the Universal Copyright Convention (as revised on July 24, 1971). These rights and subject matter take effect in the relevant jurisdiction in which the License terms are sought to be enforced according to the corresponding provisions of the implementation of those treaty provisions in the applicable national law. If the standard suite of rights granted under applicable copyright law includes additional rights not granted under this License, such additional rights are deemed to be included in the License; this License is not intended to restrict the license of any rights under applicable law.

Lightning Source UK Ltd.
Milton Keynes UK
UKOW03f1121160415

249762UK00001B/15/P

9 785510 791785